The Exploits of Ensign Bakewell

By the same author:

Wellington at War in the Peninsula: An Overview and Guide

Wellington Invades France: The Final Phase of the Peninsular War, 1813–1814

A Commanding Presence: Wellington in the Peninsula: Logistics • Strategy • Survival

An Atlas of the Peninsular War, 1808–1814

Introduction to the first Spanish translation of *The Recollections of Rifleman Harris* and Introductions to reprints of G.R. Gleig's *The Subaltern*, and *The Private Journal of Judge-Advocate Larpent*

Los Curiosos Impertinentes: Viajeros Ingleses por España; 1760–1855

Richard Ford, 1796–1858: Hispanophile, Connoisseur and Critic

The Exploits of
Ensign Bakewell

With the Inniskillings
in the Peninsula, 1810–11;
& in Paris, 1815

Edited by Ian Robertson

FRONTLINE BOOKS, LONDON

The Exploits of Ensign Bakewell: With the Inniskillings in the Peninsula, 1810–11;
& in Paris, 1815

This edition published in 2012 by Frontline Books,
an imprint of Pen & Sword Books Ltd,
47 Church Street, Barnsley, S. Yorkshire, S70 2AS
www.frontline-books.com

ISBN: 978-1-84832-698-9

For more information on our books, please visit
www.frontline-books.com, email info@frontline-books.com
or write to us at the above address.

Printed and bound by CPI Group (UK) Ltd, Croydon, CR0 4YY

Typeset in 13/14.5 point Perpetua by JCS Publishing Services Ltd
www.jcs-publishing.co.uk

Contents

Illustrations

Maps and Plans

Bakewell's route when advancing from Ostend to Paris, as described in Chapter 16, ran directly via Bruges to Ghent before turning due south to Mons, there veering south-west to Péronne, from which it continued straight to Paris.

His return to the Channel coast (Chapter 19) followed almost precisely the same route, with only very minor detours, largely due to the congestion of the roads.

Prologue

ROBERT BAKEWELL'S DIARIES WOULD NEVER have been published had not their editor, Ian Robertson, walked into my office in Beauchamp Place, near Knightsbridge, some forty-five years ago. The precise purpose of his visit was one that I can no longer remember, but I do know that, during the brief time that he spent with me, his eye was caught by the proof copies of the jacket for a book that I was preparing to publish. It was to be an edition of the manuscript diaries of a veteran of Wellington's campaigns in the Peninsula. Being particularly interested in the Peninsular War, as I was, Ian asked if I could let him have one of the jackets, and I was only too happy to oblige.

The discovery of the dairies was partly due to the fact that, in the early 'fifties, I had served as a commissioned officer in Bakewell's old regiment, the Inniskilling Fusiliers, or, as they were known in his time, the 27th Regiment of Foot. One of the oldest regiments in the British Army, it had been founded in 1689 at the time of the siege of Enniskillen (to give it its modern spelling) by the forces of James II prior the decisive battle of the Boyne. It had fought in most of the wars of the eighteenth century, and then in the Peninsula, before participating in the battle of Waterloo. There, it had formed square near the centre of the Allied line to resist Ney's cavalry attacks on that steaming hot Sunday afternoon in June 1815, in which, badly mauled, and suffering heavy casualties, it had won the admiration of both Wellington and Napoleon alike.

In 1965 I had formed my own publishing company, and of course eager to find fresh new material. I happened to notice in one of the regimental publications that were sent to me from time to time as an ex-officer, that the regimental museum had the custody of the Bakewell manuscript diaries, which aroused my curiosity. I wrote and asked if the Regiment would allow me to peruse them, and they very kindly did so. I can still remember the thrill I felt as I pored through the musty pages of the notebooks in which they had been written, and travelled in time back to the Napoleonic wars. Here, I felt, was the raw material of history.

Laced with humour and irony — though often touchingly naïve — Bakewell's accounts of his marches, the actions in which he fought, and the privations he suffered, have an immediacy that endears him to the reader even if they shed no light on the strategy of the campaigns; but they do provide — as few historians can — the sense of actually 'being there'. Of great interest also, as being a subject rarely described, are Bakewell's account of his experiences during the Allied occupation of Paris after the debacle of Waterloo. Naturally, I was elated when the Regiment gave me permission to publish these diaries. I felt that I had a 'hit' on my hands. But then things went wrong. I was under-capitalized: I made misjudgements: then suddenly the publishing company that I had founded with such high hopes, ceased to exist.

Great, however, was my surprise when the telephone rang some months ago, and — out of the blue — I found myself speaking to Ian Robertson again, whom I had hardly seen more than twice since that day in 1967 when we first met. By chance, the book jacket that I had given him all those years ago had come to light among his 'archives'; and having in recent years written and edited other books on that war, he was curious to know why the Bakewell Diaries had never been published. When I explained what had happened, he said that he might well be interested in editing them for publication himself. So I referred him to the Regimental Museum, and was delighted when he later rang to tell me that he had succeeded in obtaining a copy of the original typescript which had been prepared at the time.

I can now congratulate him on the excellent job he has done in editing them. It is truly thrilling to know that Bakewell's diaries have finally made their way into print.

Peter Dawnay

Foreword, and Acknowledgements

THIS CONTRIBUTION TO THE NUMBER of Peninsular War narratives which have come to light in recent decades has been edited on the assumption that the reader is reasonably familiar already with both the history of the period and the progress of the war.

However, for their ease, I have felt obliged to take several liberties, particularly in the case of the author's idiosyncratic punctuation, and have divided up endless pages of unbroken text into paragraphs and chapters. A number of tediously dull, entirely inconsequential passages, and repetitions, have been silently deleted, and a deal of extraneous matter and mere 'padding' has been jettisoned. Spelling has been corrected, as have several topographical and personal names, etc., while Christian names have been added where known. On many occasions I have had little alternative but to re-write Robert Bakewell's stilted and laboured, prose – one might well describe it as early nineteenth century 'Red Brick' English – sometimes barely comprehensible; but I have endeavoured throughout to retain in substance both his general tone and meaning. Without intending to weigh down the following pages with needless apparatus – dotting all the Is and crossing all the Ts – I have added a certain number of footnotes, which I hope may be of some value or interest.

Bakewell's text contains several curiosities; for instance, he never penned the word 'church', which always appears as 'chapel': perhaps he was a Methodist; and he always writes vedette (a mounted sentry), when picket or picquet (a small body of men on guard at an outpost) would have been more appropriate. His habitual inclusion of precise times of day, dates, and distances (however much they may pall) may be found useful to the military historian; and would confirm that a high proportion of his text was written from notes jotted in a diary at the time. Bakewell does not conceal his penchant for *Les Parisiennes* – though not as coarsely as might August Schaumann,[1] his contemporary – for dancing, and for food and drink, even listing what he consumed; while the record of the cost of provisions is of interest also, as likewise are his caustic comments on the rites of the Roman Catholic Church, on burials, the inadequacies of the medical profession in general, or the incompetence and ineffectiveness of Spanish regular troops and their commanders.

One 'revisionist' historian has attempted to rehabilitate the long-held image of the British rank-and-file of the period, a certain proportion of whom Wellington had castigated as being 'scum of the earth', but it should be realised that such opprobrious words – perfectly apt in the circumstances, for they were by no means always angels – are almost always quoted entirely out of context. But as an enlightened reviewer of this thesis has trenchantly remarked, its author had made 'little use of the General Orders or court martial records which provide more reliable evidence than later memoirs.'

It is doubtless a sign of the times that in recent years there has been a ridiculous and indeed most misleading sophism disseminated – flying in the face of all reliable evidence – which is that the operations of Spanish armies contributed far more to the successful outcome of the Peninsular War than in fact

---

1   As frequently evident in his *On the Road with Wellington*.

was so, while the participation of the Anglo-Portuguese army is slighted. Certainly, no one would deny that the embodiment of many thousands of Portuguese troops (having once been properly trained and commanded by British officers seconded to their army) was materially invaluable; but we are referring here to ostensibly disciplined armies, not to the peasantry and civil population in general.

While the presence of Spanish armies tied down substantial French forces over a long period, and the irregular activities of partisans, or *guerrilleros*, whether in spirited or passive opposition to the invader, caused them considerable annoyance, keeping significant numbers of troops engaged in the thankless task of protecting their inevitably extended lines of communication, their exploits should not be stressed any more than those of professed regular armies.

The revisionist clique has even floated the idea that, because the overall casualties suffered by Spanish armies – killed, wounded, missing (or deserted) – were numerically far greater than the losses of their allies (which is true enough), the same proportion of emphasis should be devoted to the battles, encounters, sorties, raids, interceptions, ambushes, and skirmishes in which the Spanish clashed with the French in any way, however unimportant. This proposition has even spilled over into the decision to describe these actions at unwarranted length in the text and to provide an inordinate number of maps and plans in at least one book that has come my way, in which it has been pontificated that 'What saved the Allied cause in the Peninsula was therefore not Wellington's genius but rather Napoleon's errors', even if adding in mitigation, 'This, however, is not to decry the British commander's very real contribution to the Allied cause', for which condescension we are indeed grateful. The present author, when once making tribute to the occasional successes of British forces in that conflict, was even charged with 'triumphalism': any such derogatory comments can only be treated with deserved derision.

But we now live in a make-believe world in which the absurd conceit of 'political correctness' is only too evident – not only in paltry attempts to re-write military history and make it more palatable: this surfeit of hypocritical humbug should be resisted vigorously whenever imposed, let alone merely voiced.

It should be emphasised that actual combats occupied far less than five per cent of the time; and also that by 1814 the contesting armies had been exposed to several years of marching and foraging (both for themselves and for their mounts), or merely subsisting as best they could, whether it be under a blistering summer sun, in torrential rain, freezing winds or a blanket of snow. The vagaries of the climate in the Peninsula are extreme. Indeed, the imagination must be well stretched in this enervated twenty-first century to appreciate properly the stamina and fortitude essential to survive the harsh conditions: officers and men had to be very tough, both physically and mentally, whether fighting for their lives or supporting the tedium of long, bleak, and bitter winters.[2]

In several instances, I have been obliged to recourse to the inclusion of editorial sections, printed in italic, when Bakewell's narrative has been either too confused, too fragmentary, or requires amplification. When editing, no

---

2   *An Atlas of the Peninsular War* (Yale University Press, ISBN 978-0-300-14869-5), containing superb cartography in colour by Martin Brown, provides both the clearest and most accurate representation of the contour and terrain of the Peninsula and south-western France, and the major actions and movements in which the Anglo-Portuguese army under Wellington were engaged, Spanish units participating in some of them.

attempt has been made to impose consistency in the way Bakewell recorded distances, measurements, etc., for which, and for any other lingering infelicities, the reader's indulgence is sought.

In his foreword to 'The Peninsular War Journals of Lieutenant Charles Crowe', entitled *An Eloquent Soldier*, Gareth Glover remarked that only very few narratives of that period by members of the Inniskillings have survived: those of Francis Simcoe, John Emerson, and William Brooke; thus anything of the nature of this present title, filling out and complementing the record of the 27th Foot, is of interest, however different may be the intrinsic value of their texts.[3]

Naturally, I am greatly indebted to Gareth in particular, but I must also list the following for a variety of reasons, among them that of providing moral support: Jack Dunlop, Curator of the Inniskillings Museum, and Richard Bennett; Gerald Dalby, for kindly allowing me to reproduce the only known portrait of Robert Bakewell; also Michael Ayrton, Rudolph Bakker, Peter Barnes, Thomas Bean, Martin Brown, Andrew Cormack, Michael Crumplin, Peter Dawnay, Nicholas Dunne-Lynch, Andrew Hewson, John Houlding, Martin Howard, John Hussey, Conrad Kent, John Lewis, Hugh Logan, Rory Muir, Janet and Derwent Renshaw, Delia Richards; and – not least – my wife, Marie-Thérèse. I must also thank Stephen Chumbley for his sound editorial advice and assistance during the preparation of these pages for the press.

The illustrations reproduced have been accumulated over many years, and although the sources are indicated after their captions in several instances, I have been unable to establish these in each case. While every effort has been made to obtain permission to use what may be copyright material, the author

---

3   See the Selective Bibliography for details.

and publishers apologise for any errors or omissions, and would be grateful to be notified of any corrections that should be incorporated in a reprint or revised edition.

Arles, 1 November 2011

π

Introduction:
Bakewell's Youth

ROBERT BAKEWELL WAS BORN ON 20 September 1775 into a family of yeoman farmers at Castle Donington, a village in Leicestershire half-way between Loughborough and Derby. The family was related to Robert Bakewell (1725–95) of Dishley Grange, near Loughborough, famous in his day as a livestock breeder. Young Robert was one of eight children born to Thomas and Ann Bakewell.[1] Of their three daughters and five sons, two daughters and a son had died by 1800. Apparently, at a later date, there was some disagreement over the distribution of property, and this rankled with young Robert; indeed he considered that he had been excluded from the division of 'the spoil amongst themselves', as he described it in his rambling reminiscences.

This manuscript, elaborately entitled 'The history and the life of the author, stating the most incidental and casual occurrences, and other occasional matter, in order to elucidate the completion of the following narrative and descriptive statement of facts,' was probably written up in the mid or late 1820s. By then, Bakewell was living with his sister Ann at Hall Farm House, No. 9 High Street, Castle Donington,[2] which dated from 1634.

---

1   Thomas Bakewell died on 27 June 1819, aged 76, while Ann, his wife, the daughter of Henshaw Briggs, Gent., died on 7 December 1831, aged 84.
2   Young Ann died in 1862, aged 72.

Bakewell gives little information about his 'early and infantine days,' merely referring to the fact that he was a 'weakly boy, and occasionally subject to fits', although he daily gained health and strength with years. We are told that as there were 'three of four of us boys at home, which no doubt gave trouble,' his parents had sent them to school early, 'more for their conveniency to have us out of the way, than for any learning that we could acquire.' They were later sent to Mr Whyman's academy at neighbouring Aston, where 'his system of instruction was very different from any other practise'; for 'he never used to beat any of his scholars; and was always introducing something new, in order to stimulate them to exertion and emulation.' Bakewell mentions that 'Perry's *Dictionary* was at all times our guide for spelling and pronouncing,'[3] and that, in the former, he 'was always at the top of the first class.' He could have hardly claimed such ability as far as both his grammar was concerned, however well grounded he may have assumed his vocabulary might have been. Although not highly educated, Bakewell knew how to give expression to his wry sense of humour even if he had little natural talent for writing. It is not known to what extent he may have jotted down any memoranda at the actual time of his experiences, and it is unfortunate that, when returning to them at a later date, he felt compelled to incorporate a deal of extraneous material to provide context and pad out the text, which only detracted from the vigour of his first-hand narrative.

When aged fourteen, Bakewell was 'bound' as apprentice to a linen draper at Derby but, before very long, circumstances forced him to accept a variety of alternative employments until the spring of 1797, when he was 'engaged' in his first 'London

---

3   William Perry's *Royal Standard English Dictionary* was first published in 1775.

servitude', which lasted for several years. There is little indication that he ever contemplated a military career, although during what he described as being a period in which the citizens were 'attacked with a military frenzy,' he was inevitably drawn into it. Ten City Regiments had been formed, and Bakewell and a colleague entered the 5th Loyal London, which drilled regularly in the Blue Coat Hospital Yard, conveniently near his lodgings. Here, in the summer, the volunteers devoted two hours each morning (except Sundays) to 'handling the musket', while twice a week they marched to Islington at 2 o'clock 'for the purpose of firing ball cartridges' at a distance of one hundred yards from their targets. In 1803, all the city volunteers were taken to Hyde Park for one of several inspections, where Lord Harrington drilled them 'by marching and counter-marching for three or four hours before they were complimented and dismissed'.[4] Several similar inspections took place, memorable being that attended by the king together with a number of generals, when several of these 'these soldier citizens', while returning down Bird Cage Walk, fell down exhausted, having been kept on the field for six hours; others fell out and 'repaired to the pastry cooks', leaving their ranks 'greatly thinned'.

After seven years in London, most of the time being employed in the haberdashery or calico trade and also with Russia merchants, in every case without great advancement, and suffering from the financial failure of some of his masters (not all of whom were too honest), unable to establish himself and thoroughly disillusioned, Bakewell packed his bags and returned to Castle Donington. Unfortunately, the prospects of employment there were no better, nor were his family as

---

4   General Charles Stanhope, third Earl Harrington (1753–1829), whose seat was Elvaston Castle, between Shardlow and Derby

hospitable as he might have expected them to be: indeed, all the world seemed to be conspiring against him.

However, the parish vicar, the Revd John Dalby,[5] who had married Mary Ann Bakewell, his father's niece, was also chaplain to the Earl of Moira.[6] On one fine day, an acquaintance remarked to Bakewell that he had seen his name 'gazetted for an Ensigncy commission in the 27th Regiment', the Inniskillings.[7] This was surprising news: until then, he was unaware that his father had paid Dalby £400 to pass on to Lord Moira.[8] Bakewell had also just received a letter from a certain George Sills, offering an Ensigncy in the same regiment for only £250. However, he was 'glad to get away on any terms', and on writing in 13 May to his Lordship for instructions, was ordered to report to Ballyshannon in Ireland, the Depot of the 27th.[9] In his reply, Lord Moira had enclosed letters addressed to Major William Brydges Neynoe,[10]

---

5   The Revd John Dalby (1771–1852), was vicar of Castle Donington from 1807. His elder brother, Thomas (1768–1849) was an attorney there (as was his father, also Thomas), and acted as agent for the Moira estates from 1813, when Lord Moira was in India as Governor-General of Bengal.

6   Francis Rawdon-Hastings (1754–1826) succeeded as second Earl of Moira in 1793, becoming Marquis of Hastings in 1817. Born in Ireland, and educated at Harrow and Oxford, he had joined the army in 1771, and served in the American War of Independence. His seat, Donington Hall, was built in 1790–93 by William Wilkins the Elder. Moira was also colonel of the 27th, a very popular regiment, of three battalions, and with the 18th, one of the two officially titled 'Irish regiments,' although a high proportion of the 87th, and 88th (the Connaught Rangers) were also Irishmen.

7   Dated 12 April 1810.

8   £400 was the current cost of purchasing a commission as Ensign (£900, if in the Foot Guards).

9   In the event, his brother George having been suddenly taken seriously ill, Bakewell had applied for leave to delay his departure, which Moira had granted.

10   Major William Brydges Neynoe (1767–1835), who was referred to by

commanding there, 'to request his kindness towards you', and to Messrs Atkinsons, the regiment's agent at Ely Place, Dublin. The latter 'will put you in the way of furnishing yourself with your uniform and the other articles which you ought to have in joining the Regiment and I am sure they will be happy in offering you their civilities.' Bakewell's father gave him £120 with which to equip himself 'with necessary trappings, etc.'

Curiously, Bakewell hardly refers to any campaigns or combats which had taken place in the Peninsula during the previous twenty months, ever since Lieutenant General Sir Arthur Wellesley had first landed with an expeditionary force at the mouth of the Mondego, on the Atlantic coast of Portugal. No mention is made of the battle of Vimeiro, the outcome of which was the evacuation from Lisbon of Junot's army of occupation; nor of Sir John Moore's unfortunate winter campaign, which ended with the evacuation of his army from Corunna.[11] It is difficult to know to what extent the general public – other than the citizens of London, or Portsmouth, Plymouth, and similar military and naval centres – were aware of the progress of the war. Even when serving with the 27th Regiment in Ireland prior to embarking for the Peninsula, Bakewell is also silent about more recent events, such as Masséna's seizure of Ciudad Rodrigo early in July at the commencement of his army's advance into Portugal, although news of this second French invasion of Portugal must have filtered through in the papers, avidly read by all officers in the regimental depot in Ireland.

Lieutenant Charles Crowe at a later date as being pompous and self-important.
11   The 3rd Battalion of the Inniskillings had not fought at Corunna, having been sent directly south to form part of Lieutenant General Sir John Craddock's force defending Lisbon, being stationed at Sacavém on the estuary of the Tagus.

I

In the Peninsula, 1810–11

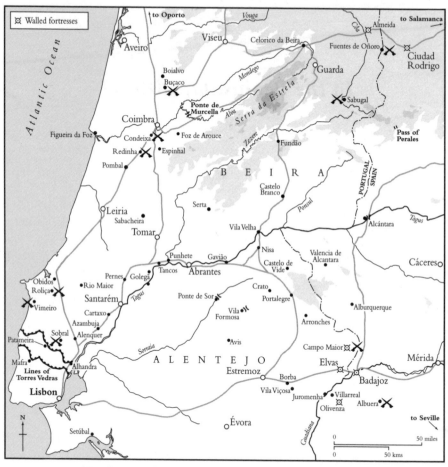

Map 1: Central Portugal and the abutting frontier of Spain
referred to by Bakewell

CHAPTER 1

On Joining the 27th

I QUIT CASTLE DONINGTON ON 26 June, 1810, and certainly at that time I had little prospect of seeing or returning to it again. I took the telegraph coach at Cavendish Bridge; it changed horses at Derby, Leek, and Macclesfield, and reached Manchester that same evening. Next morning I called on a few friends employed in the manufactories in this town and at 1 o'clock I boarded a coach for Liverpool, changing horses at Warrington; but as I had no business or friends there of any moment, I took the first opportunity of securing my passage on the *Earl of Moira* packet for Dublin. It sailed on the following day, the 28th, and was forty-eight hours on the passage, a very rough one, during which I was seasick for the first and only time in my life. Altogether, it was not a very unpleasant journey, although they were several agreeable Paddys in the cabin with me.

We landed at the Pigeon House (Dublin) on the 30th, and I drove directly to *Flannagan's Hotel* in Dawson Street. It was at *Richmond's Hotel* next door that I drank the best bottle of porter I ever tasted, despite having lived in London several years. After a meal, I called on Mr Atkinson, the Irish agent of the 27th Regiment, and delivered my credentials. He invited me to dine with him that day, a Saturday, and likewise on the Monday, but as I had planned to set off next day, being anxious to report at the Depot; and also wanted see as much as possible of Dublin as time would allow, I excused myself.

On my return to the inn, by chance I met a Mr James Hart, who, about six months previously, had dined at my father's and who immediately recognised me. He insisted that I must moved from the inn to his house in Kildare Street, nor would he leave me until I had instructed a porter to take my luggage there, where I spent the evening and slept well. On the following day, after breakfast with his son John, who now holds a Lieutenancy in the 12th Regiment, we took a ride round the city (what they term the circle) in a gig. Dublin contains a good many buildings, such as the College, the Bank, the Castle, etc., and is a compact, well built town for its size. As I was unable to leave that day, after dinner we strolled through most of the principal streets, and I stayed a second night.

I set out for Ballyshannon next morning, taking the coach for Sligo, which passed through Chapelizod, Lucan, Leixlip, Kilcock, and Clonard, and I slept at Mullingar, continuing next day through Newton Forbes, Roosky, Drumsna, Jamestown, Carrick-on-Shannon, Boyle, and Collooney.

On the following morning there was a great cattle-fair in Sligo, for all types: cows, sheep, horses, etc.; it was also a considerable market for wool, though the stock was much inferior to that usually exhibited at similar events in England, being much smaller and very lean. It was here that I first saw a fight between two Irish peasants, who laid on lustily, wielding sticks some four to five feet in length, what they termed a shilaly [shillelagh], and considerably disfigured each others' heads. I stayed at Sligo until midday, when I hired a post chaise for Ballyshannon, as there were no coaches or wagons on these cross roads. The distance was twenty-two Irish miles or twenty-eight English (eleven Irish miles being almost exactly fourteen English).

I reached Ballyshannon at 4.0 in this conveyance – more like a lumbering coach than a chaise – and put up at the inn.

Next morning, I delivered my testimonials to Major Neynoe, commanding at the Depot,[1] who introduced me to the other officers of the 27th Regiment stationed there: Captain Bevan, Lieutenants Richard Shaw and John Doris, Ensign Martin McLeod, and assistant surgeon Kennedy. On the major's recommendation, I took lodgings with a Mr Boyle; and joined the mess next day: this was small, there being only seven of us; but as the room was in Mr Boyle's house, I had no great distance to go from my bed to my dinner.

Ballyshannon has a market on a Saturday, attended by about three thousand people. Being on the coast, it is well supplied with fish, particularly salmon, and the officers often amused themselves with fly-fishing when not on duty; and as Lieutenant Doris would take nine or ten salmon each week, averaging 14 or 15 lb each, his success gave us great encouragement.[2] Billiards was a game much played by the officers.

Their usual beverage was wine with dinner, and whiskey in the evening. Poteen whiskey is an illicit spirit, much of it

---

1   The barracks there had been erected by 1710.

2   Bakewell described Ballyshannon as a town 'well known for what is generally termed a salmon leap. At the entrance there is a fall of water of from 7 to 12 feet (as the descent depends upon the tide ebbing to and fro) into the sea, and it is a pretty sight of a fine day to see the salmon, by twisting their tails, jump at least 10 feet above the surface, and then swim along a shallow rivulet and against a strong current for several hundred yards, when those from 10 to 30 lb each may be pulled out with the greatest of ease with a kind of shark hook. I suppose this fishery must supply more salmon than any other in Europe. They retail here at 3d per lb, and carried to Dublin (100 miles distant) to sell for 6d per lb. There are seven or eight men constantly on the lookout during the season, stationed in a small boat, from which, when they see the water troubled, they throw out their nets and haul in quantities. I have seen them count 183 at one draught, averaging 13 or 14 lb each; while at other times their catch may be from four to seven score.'

being made in the neighbourhood, and drunk here in quantity. Our mess used to buy it at 7/- per gallon. The suppliers would bring along their full kegs at midnight and collect the empties together with the cash. For the first month at least, I did not think this whiskey at all palatable: everything I eat or drank appeared to be smoked, due to them burning turf and not coal to cook with, but in time I was inured to that kind of spirit and liked it better, and latterly I would rather have taken a tumbler of poteen punch, than of wine. I don't mean the licensed spirit, but the illicit spirit made by the locals, more genuine and not intermixed with those nauseous ingredients as is that produced by the public distilleries.

The players were at Ballyshannon while I was there, and they were well supported. Also, at *Flannagan's Hotel*, balls were got up frequently for the entertainment of both officers and local families, and well attended and pleasant ones they were. Both card-parties and oyster-eatings were much in vogue at this time.

There does not appear to be that delicacy observed here between the different sexes, as in England. During my first week I went to have a bathe, the sea being close by, and I had not been in the water for five minutes when I noticed a Mrs Lipsitt – a buxom-looking linen-draper's wife – undressing not ten yards away from me; but at least she donned her bathing gown on before plunging in. I found this to be the general custom; while at Bundoran, about three miles to the west, which is what they term a fashionable watering-place for the quality during the summer season, both sexes (at least, of the peasantry) plunge into the sea in crowds, intermixed and as naked as they were born, and apparently as much unconcerned as if they were no females amongst them.

I lodged with Mr Boyle for two months, when I moved into barracks, where each officer has two rooms (a bed and a sitting one) with a small amount of furniture, unless there is an overflow of officers, when they sometimes double them up, placing two subalterns in the same rooms. Some of the officers carry their beds with them; otherwise, they hire them from the local tradesmen, paying a weekly sum. Canteens are a useful article in the Service. I had a pair containing breakfast and dinner service for four, with kettles, frying pans, candle sticks, etc., while the barrack-master furnished us with fire irons, bellows, chairs, tables, etc., and a supply of coals and candles. With these essential utensils, and a servant at their command, the officers have a very comfortable time.

A variety of girls visit us in the barracks; some would even come thirty or forty miles distant, and stay three or four days and then leave; some return, but this depends to a great extent on the encouragement they previously received; however, the numbers that do visit provides a wide choice to the barrack residents.

*

Bakewell later remarked that, while at Ballyshannon, he wrote to Lord Moira: 'There being a vacancy of the situation of Paymaster in the first battalion of your Lordship's regiment, if you without inconveniencing yourself could secure that appointment in my favour, I should ever feel myself much obliged for your assistance, and beg your Lordship to accept my best thanks for the trouble you have already taken on me entering my military career of life.' Bakewell's application for the post was unsuccessful.

*

When I had been here about three weeks, a detachment of 200 men was to be forwarded to the 3rd Battalion of the 27th, at that time stationed in Portugal (the 1st and the 2nd battalions being then in Italy). These three battalions were alternately reinforced from the Depot, whenever they required an additional strength; and this particular detachment, when added to the 3rd, caused it to be very strong: more than 1,100 rank and file.[3] An order was then received by our commanding officer to march them away by the 14th of September, previous to which there was a general inspection.

Those being selected set off at 5.0 that morning, divided into three companies in charge of Lieutenant Doris, assisted by Ensign Hare and myself, and we each commanded and paid one of them. It being a fine morning, we had a pleasant although long march to Enniskillen, a distance of twenty-five Irish miles; but our destination was Cork, a distance of over 200 miles across country. On the day we left Ballyshannon, we breakfasted at Church Hill, and reached Enniskillen at 3 o'clock.

One might mention here that Major Neynoe had informed this detachment that one man out of every twenty would be permitted to take his wife with him to the Peninsula, and that is half a score for the whole three companies. I suppose that about one third or so were married, but if more than this number accompanied them to Cork, they would have to cast lots which should go.[4] Fifty or so of these damsels had joined us, but our first days march reduced their number by at least ten.

The 90th Regiment being stationed in Enniskillen, their officers sent an invitation to those of the 27th to dine with them, but we excused ourselves as one of ours, whose name was Batty,[5] there on the recruiting service, was providing a

---

3   The 27th was almost the largest regiment in the army: Oman list 3,448 officers and men being on the establishment on July 1809.

4   Regulations allowed the rank and file to take only six wives per company on campaign. The wives of officers, at their own expense, might accompany their husbands without any such restriction.

5   In all probability this was John Aspine Batty, a lieutenant in 1806.

dinner for us. But as our party was small — there being only three officers — for neither Doris nor William Hare had yet joined the detachment, Batty gave us a good dinner and lots of the necessary afterwards, and we spent a pleasant evening.

At dawn, preceded by bugle-calls, to give notice of our approach, we walked eight miles to Maguire's Bridge, where we breakfasted, and halted that day and the following. Lieutenant Armstrong, who was stationed here on recruiting service also, introduced me to the Graham family, where we took tea and spent the evening with Mrs and the Miss Grahams, the clergyman and doctor of the parish joining us. Lieutenant Richard Shaw followed us here from Ballyshannon on his tandem,[6] proposing to give us occasional lifts on the road; but we told him that there was no need. Mrs Graham gave me a letter for her son, who was a lieutenant in the 27th stationed in Portugal.

On Monday the 17th we left Maguire's Bridge and proceeded seven miles to Newton Butler, where we met Lieutenant George Pratt, who was recruiting there and had breakfast in readiness for us, after which we continued to Cavan, eleven miles beyond.[7] The officers of the 21st Regiment were stationed here, and invited us to join their mess, but our duties interfering, we dined at the inn.

We left Cavan on Tuesday 18 September and proceeded four miles to Bellanagh, where we breakfasted, and reached Granard for dinner. Next day we had a short march to Edgesworth

---

6   A tandem in this sense being two horses harnessed behind each other.

7   Bakewell observed that the Earl of Farnham had a noble mansion and extensive parks here (it lies a short distance west of Cavan); while at Enniskillen, the county town for Fermanagh, stood the castle of the Earl of that name, brother to General The Hon. Galbraith Lowry Cole, and also the mansion (Caslecoole) of the Earl of Belmore.

Town, only seven miles away, where we halted until the 20th, when we marched another ten to Ballimahon.

During the next few days our route, bypassing Athlone, continued through Ferbane (a nineteen-mile march), Cloghan, and Birr, commonly called Parsonstown,[8] where we halted. The Galway regiment of Militia was stationed here, and we were sent an invitation by their adjutant to dine with them, but we excused ourselves. As it was Sunday, the adjutant called on us again, repeating the invitation in the name of Lord Clancarty and the officers of the regiment,[9] which we then accepted and went to their mess to enjoy a plentiful dinner and a variety of delicious wines, and spent a very pleasant evening.

On the morning of the 24th we progressed to Roscrea, a distance of nine miles. I noticed a kind of monument here, one of many in this part of the country, which – so I was told – were erected by the Druids as places of worship many centuries since: it was even said that it was built before the birth of our Saviour. It is about 12 or 14 yards in circumference, and is quite high.

Next day we marched via Temple More to Thurles on the river Suir, where there is a nunnery and one of the more elegant Catholic churches I have seen since my arrival in Ireland.

On the following morning, after three and a half miles, we reached a hamlet called the Holy Cross, and halted in order to examine the ruins of an abbey that had once covered an acre of ground, and likewise said to have been completed a century before the birth of Christ; and apparently one of their ancient monarchs was interred here, part of an inscription being still

---

8   The land had been granted to Laurence Parsons in 1620.
9   Richard Le Poer Trench, usually referred to as the Earl of Clancarty (1767–1837), then colonel of the Galway Militia.

visible. But what was formerly Holy Cross Abbey was now completely gutted, though the curtain walls were still standing at almost their original height, from 79 to 80 feet. We climbed to the highest part, which provided an extensive view from this county of Tipperary into the adjoining ones.

Afterwards, we entered Cashel, a distance of seven miles and, on arriving early, breakfasted and walked round the town, on the east side of which is a hill from the summit of which the counties of Queens, Carlow and Wexford may be seen. We examined the ruins of what was formerly a cathedral, where we found an ancient and curious collection of monuments set up as memorials to the priests and bishops interred there; and many underground passages still remain in the interior, but the outer walls are much decayed, although some of the corners survive at their original height, being from 140 to 150 feet.

On our return to the inn we met the adjutant of the Fermanagh Militia, who invited us to their mess; and we accepted the invitation, having first seen all our men settled into good billets. They gave us an excellent dinner with the usual wines, and having taken our fill, we departed at 10 o'clock after being pleasantly entertained.

As I was passing along a street, I heard music and saw dancing in one of the houses. Supposing it to be a public dance, I went to ask, only to be told that it was a private house and a wedding had just taken place. I apologised for the intrusion and was about to retire, but as it was the bride who met me at the door and proposed I should dance with her, I could not well refuse, and so we danced for fifteen minutes, footing it by ourselves. She then took me to an adjoining room, where a catholic priest and about eighty guests, male and female, were sitting on long benches round several tables, drinking some of the best poteen punch, served in jugs containing a gallon each, to which I helped myself plentifully. As refreshments were in abundance, I stayed here playing with the girls and carousing with the company until 5.0 next day, when the bugles signalled the detachment's departure, at which I took my leave. I lost my watch here, but having a quantity of money with me (what with my own and the pay of the men) made me more than anxious to preserve the whole amount; the loss of the watch (which I never saw again) was a secondary consideration, although I left the number and the maker's name with the officers of the Fermanagh.[10]

We then set off to Cahir, where there are ruins of an old castle, and continued our march for Clogheen. After about five miles we met the largest Irish funeral I had ever witnessed, led by almost eighty women, the front row carrying what appeared to be a large kite, placed at the top of a staff 12 or 13 feet in length, decorated all over with military plumes. The rest walked in pairs, each with an olive branch. Behind them came some eighty or more men in their shirt sleeves and with white muslin handkerchiefs tied round their hats. Then followed the coffin (which bore the name of a Miss Stapleton) and a crowd of men, women and children, who made most hideous sound, what they term the Irish cry: the whole party must have consisted of four or five hundred. I followed the cortege to the place of interment, where, before they committed the body to the ground, they took the lid off the coffin and exposed the corpse.

We reached Clogheen just in time for dinner, where Sampson joined us, the first officer I met of the 27th Regiment that was to accompanied me to Spain. The following morning we proceeded twelve miles to Kilworth for breakfast, and then on to Fermoy, arriving there in time for dinner. Being one of the

------

10   Bakewell soon acquired another watch, being a stickler for giving precise times!

race days, it was very full of company, many of quality among them. There was a ball at *Hone's Hotel* that evening, which, being asked to make up a party, I attended and found there an elegant assemblage of the fashionables, together with numerous officers of the 5th and 76th Regiments. I amused myself with two or three agreeable partners until 4.0 in the morning, when I retired; and had just time to change my clothes before the detachment set off again.

We reached Carigtohill after a fifteen-mile march, and our destination, the Cove [Cobh],[11] soon after, and immediately embarked on board HMS *Mercury* frigate (formerly with 28 guns, but now only 18), commanded by Captain John Tancock. What with dancing the previous night, and marching the two preceding days, I was tired out, and I slept on board very soundly.

Captain Moore took command of the detachment after the embarkation, where Phillips and McCoard joined us;[12] these three, with Sampson and I being the only five officers of the 27th that went to the Peninsula on this occasion. Doris, who came with us, returned to our Depot, as he was the acting adjutant there. Hare, an officer who had marched all the way

---

11   Cobh, or the Cove of Cork (known as Queenstown from 1849 to 1922) was an extensive natural harbour no great distance south-east of Cork. It had served as a naval base and place of concentration for the huge convoys required during the French and American wars, and several defensive forts had been built in the vicinity in the 1780s under the aegis of General Charles Vallencey (c. 1726–1812). It was from here that Sir Arthur Wellesley had set sail for the Peninsula on 12 July 1808 in command of the British expeditionary force at the commencement of the British involvement in the war. He had sailed hence also in June 1794 for Ostend, commanding the 33rd Regiment in Lord Moira's expedition).

12   Ensigns Robert Jocelyn Phillips and James McCoard, both of whom were later wounded at Badajoz, the latter mortally.

with us, declined to embark, saying he was not well; so a Lieutenant Wiltshire, belonging to another regiment, obtained his passage out.

The following morning, Sunday 30 September, I disembarked, hired a horse, and rode to Cork, a distance of eight miles, where I stayed until Tuesday evening at an inn with the other officers of the 27th, except for one who remained with the detachment on board. This duty was taken alternately, and my turn happened to be the first. While at Cork, I attended the district Pay Office, and they gave us one month's pay in advance – to the 24th of the following month. I likewise applied for the customary allowances, that is, for embarkation, and marching allowances, lodging money, etc., but all to no purpose.

CHAPTER 2

From the Cove of Cork to Lisbon

I LEFT CORK ON TUESDAY evening, 2 October, for the Cove, where I re-embarked, and remained aboard till the 4th.[1] Then, the wind being favourable, the *Mercury*, conveying four other sail for Lisbon, cleared the harbour. The voyage was rather a pleasant one, for Captain Tancock was a right good fellow with whom I spent many entertaining hours; but the fun did not last long, for McCoard was to become a great nuisance, which I little anticipated. However, we proceeded amongst calms and squalls until the 13th, when the *Catherine* brig from Liverpool lost her fore-top mast, and as she could not continue her journey alone, our vessel was lashed to her for the next two days, during which repairs were made good, when she separated, and she remained manageable for the rest of the trip. Nevertheless, two men fell from her masts: one overboard and never seen again; the other on deck, though not much hurt; while, from ours, one named John Bloomfield fell likewise: the deck caught him, but his thigh was dislocated.

The captain invited several of us to dine with him throughout the voyage, gave good dinners, and sported claret, which he downed cheerfully; and we had also formed a mess, subscribing a certain sum each, at which Lieutenant Wiltshire, who was

---

1   The battle of Busaco had taken place precisely a week earlier, on 27 September.

returning from sick leave, joined us, as occasionally did the other officers on our vessel.

Our sea stock consisted chiefly of poultry, wine, spirits, tea, sugar, bread, etc., while the Irishmen took care to have lots of 'murphys' also.[2] There was no lack of biscuits and salt provisions on board. Our telescopes first decried land on 17 October, and at dusk two days later we cast anchor at the mouth of the Tagus, about seven miles distant from Lisbon.

On the morning of the 20th the sky was serene and bright, the sea completely calm, allowing us a quite magnificent view from our ship towards the city, which we could discern in the distance, rising from the sea. Craft of every types and burden crowded along both side of the estuary for four or five miles, displaying their respective colours of numerous nations: a fine sight indeed.

Captain William Moore, commanding our detachment, took a boat and steered for Lisbon, leaving McCoard, being next in seniority, in charge during his absence. He had not exercised that authority long before he became aggressive towards me, demanding that I should give the men in my company, several of whom appeared dissatisfied with what they had received, whatever sum they wanted. I refused, and told him my pay added to their own would not have satisfied them, and that those making the complaint had already received more than their due. He still insisted, threatening that he would have me confined if I did not comply. I replied that he had not the authority. On maintaining that he did, I retorted 'You lie, Sir; I will *not* advance money for them.' He turned away at once, saying that this was just what he wanted to hear. I was a young soldier, and had little idea what the consequence might be.

---

2   The usage of Irish surname 'Murphy' to describe potatoes was a very recent slang term.

At 4 o' clock on Saturday evening the *Mercury* heaved up her anchor and attempted to sail up the river, but as there was neither wind nor tide, she could not, and when endeavouring to do so, the 16-gun frigate HMS *Espiègle* came athwart her, broke her jib-boom, and twisted her bowsprit, which caused a very spirited altercation betwixt the two captains. While they were disputing, an American merchantman drifted from her anchorage and bore down on the *Mercury*, drove in her starboard round house,[3] and carried away her martingale dauphin strikers,[4] etc. This substantial damage made our captain swear that he would do his best to seize whoever commanded the American, and have him stripped, tarred, and feathered: this, I am told, is an ancient custom, although is very seldom put in practise; but we joked with the captain, telling him he had better not try, least he should have the tables turned on himself.

On Sunday, our ship made another attempt, but was as unsuccessful. She made some slight progress next morning, but then ran foul of the *Thetis* transport,[5] and I thought might damage it seriously, but she only broke her own davit, which made us think conclude that the Tagus was an unfortunate river for the *Mercury*. However, by 2.0 she reached within a mile of Belém and dropped anchor again. I was surprised to see so small boats immediately surrounding us, offering provisions and fruit for sale: the latter were very good and cheap; melons at 4d each, and grapes about the size of acorns at 3d & 4d per lb; oranges at 4d per dozen; figs etc.; and other local produce.

---

3   A round-house is a cabin on the aft part of a quarter-deck.

4   This is a small vertical spar use together with martingales (ropes) to brace a jib-boom.

5   This vessel may well have been the 36-gun HMS *Thetis*, not a transport.

(McCoard appeared quite at home: having been in this country before, he understood a smattering of the language, but as for the rest of us, we appeared as ignorant as Hottentots at the appeals to buy made by the natives.)

Captain Moore returned to us on the 22nd and resumed command. While at Belém he had received instructions to leave McCoard on board: he would not be permitted to rejoin the 27th as apparently, he had done so before in Spain, and had then been sent back to Ireland for disorderly conduct.[6]

During the evening of Wednesday the 23rd the detachment disembarked at Belém. Next morning, Ensign Robert Phillips called on me to deliver a message to from McCoard, which was that he insisted on fighting me for giving him the lie: would I appoint the hour that very morning and choose the ground on which a duel would decide the matter. My answer was that I was unacquainted with the country and any suitable ground, so I could not chose; however, as there were several officers whom I knew, as soon as I could obtain their personal attendance, a time would be agreed. Phillips pressed me to accept William Sampson for a second, as I hardly knew the other Irishmen who had embarked with me. As I thought it prudent to have somebody at hand who would see justice done and would have an interest in my reputation, and as I had some property with me, it was so agreed.

---

6   Bakewell adds that, in the event, 'after two or three months, McChord [sic] was permitted to proceed, and just arrived in time for the siege of Badajoz, where he received a shot in the thigh which proved mortal. When wounded, he was removed to Elvas, where I was stationed and he came under my jurisdiction. As the ball had lodged in the hip, they could not extract it, and it caused an attack of the spasms, and likewise mortified, and he died. I buried him, or at least got his coffin made and had him interred, which might be said to confirm the old adage, for he fell into the pit he made for me, or at least the evil fell on his own shoulders.

However, almost immediately after this, I received orders to leave the detachment just landed and take command of another, of men belonging to several different regiments, and prepare to proceed with them to the Lines.

Next day, Sampson and I took a boat and steered for Lisbon, which when seen from a distance, one might assume to be all one very tall building, only noting the error on a closer approach. This was because several ranges of buildings rose up in succession, peeping over the others, and extending for a distance of a mile at least. Their houses are either white-washed or stuccoed, and from four to seven storeys in height, each with its balcony in front, guarded by iron railings, gilt and decorated with all that fancy could imagine. There are also a great many windmills scattered about the city, which, together with all the shipping, add to the imposing panorama.

On landing, we went directly to *Latour's Hotel*, where we dined, had a great dessert, and a good supply of drink, for their fruits and wines were excellent and in abundance.[7] After this, we traversed some of the principal streets and called at the

---

7   Bakewell seemed oblivious of the situation in which the population of the capital had found themselves. In Moyle Sherer's opinion, 'Lisbon, after the first alarm, became as it were intoxicated by a strong feeling of security: there was never a period when this city was more crowded with objects of misery, or when provisions were more extravagantly dear; yet at no time had their theatres been better filled, their societies more gay and brilliant, than when seventy thousand vindictive enemies lay within sixteen miles of the city, panting for the plunder of it. It is but justice to add, that everything which prudence and humanity could suggest was done by the inhabitants of Lisbon, to alleviate the public misfortune. The port was open to all vessels laden with provisions, the magazines were filled with them, charitable institutions were set on foot, and food daily distributed to such of the fugitives as were necessitous and helpless, while labour was provided for the others. The police, too . . . was most active; and whatever secret

'Castle de Gades',[8] a term applied to one of their coffee houses. It is to these that the more genteel girls of the town resort, for it is not here as in London: they do not flaunt their wares in the streets, but flock to the coffee houses in numbers, to await the arrival of chance paramours. Some of them don't order a thing, while others will take coffee, for which they charge 4d each; but once these frail ones are provided with their beaux, the landlord expects a remuneration for their accommodation by calling for a bottle of wine or anything else more palatable to the parties concerned, after which these wantons repair with their partners to their lodgings 'where they be conveniences to cloy their loose and unrestrained habits' (to quote Bakewell's phrase precisely).[9] Sampson and I took coffee at one of these assembly or show-rooms, grog at another, at a third, wine, etc., and in this way we had an opportunity of gratifying our curiosity before returning to *Latour*'s where we slept, and indeed stayed until Tuesday.

The following evening, when we asked for our bill, they gave one charging us from two to three thousand *reis*, which high figure surprised us. On sending for the landlord, a Frenchman who could speak English fluently, he explained that the value of a *rei,* a small decimal, was worth little more than a farthing; but it was the custom to make out all their bills in *reis,* one thousand of which hardly amount 25/- worth. With this explanation, we settled the bill, and immediately returned to our detachment of the 27th on board the *Mercury,*

---

and treasonable spirit existed among the disaffected, was compelled to remain inactive and harmless.

8   Gades was the Cadiz of antiquity. This may be an oblique reference to the improbæ Gaditanæ ,and the lascivious dances for which the city was once reputed; while for Massinger a Gaditana was a strumpet.

9   See Chapter 12, footnote 13.

arriving about half an hour before their disembarkation took place, which took place with very little trouble; but I never saw anywhere more crowded with troops: it was if it was the depot for the whole army.[10]

We put our 200 men in a small part of a barracks, and once they were settled into their quarters with their provisions, the officers met back at the hotel, where we had a snack and a plenty of good wine; but as for beds there was hardly one to be had in the whole town, and it was with great with difficulty that we were able to find any. I secured three by about 2 o'clock and, being much fatigued, slept tolerably well until daylight, the landlord having given us the use of a small room to ourselves.[11]

I was provided next morning with a billet in a private house occupied by a gentleman who had previously been a captain in the Portuguese service. On presenting my billet, he showed me into the parlour in which where his wife and daughter, and welcomed me according to their custom, by kissing my cheek repeatedly, and hugging me by throwing his right arm under my left and slapping me on the back. This kissing, hugging, and slapping is their habitual way of salutation, rather than what we are used to in England, when shaking hands is the friendly way of introduction. I thought possibly this hugging system might be the convention with the ladies also, but when I approached them, the venerable captain stepped forwards and said 'No

---

10   The disembarkation took place at Belém, no great distance west of the city. Bakewell adds that apart from the effectives, at that time there were almost 10,000 sick in hospitals, not counting detachments stationed elsewhere.

11   A footnote, perhaps meant to be placed here, states: 'When I awoke, to my great surprise, instead of being with the officers of the 27th, I found myself in the barracks, quarter of a mile distant, lying beside my chest, and I never found out how I got there.'

Signor', explaining that it was not the practise to clap and kiss with females.

He then took me over to their pianoforte but I explained that as I was no musician, I could not divert myself with the instrument; so he then produced cards, and we amused ourselves by a game very much like that the ladies play at in England, called quadrille, and spent a pleasant evening together. Later, when I retired, he led me into an elegant room with a high frame above the bed, and elegant chintz trimmings; the sheets had a border of cambric muslin, and were crimped like the frill of a man's shirt, about three nails in breadth,[12] and the pillows had different coloured ribbons in bows – green, sky, purple, pink, lilac, etc. – tied round them. What with the crimped and frilled sheets, and the variegated coloured ribbons on the pillows, and other furniture to correspond, I thought myself very smartly accommodated, but during the night I was restless. Indeed, when I awoke at daylight and turned down the sheet, I saw numerous little fellows dancing to and fro: perhaps several hundred fleas. I immediately quit my roost, but I am told that in these hot countries it is almost impossible to escape them.

After breakfast, I went to parade; and, on my return, I received an order to take command of a batch of convalescents, who would be joining their respective regiments as soon as they were fit for the march; and thus my stint with the detachment with which I had disembarked, ceased.

Curiosity caused me to attend mass at a church called the Queen's,[13] recently erected, and considered an elegant one. On

---

12   His former employment had made Bakewell familiar with the names of different fabrics. A nail (2¼ in.) is an old measure for cloth lengths.

13   The present Basilica da Estrela, built by the devout and melancholy Maria I. The adjacent convent had already been put to use as a military hospital.

entering, I observed at the end of the chancel, three priests standing, very elegantly dressed – particularly the one in the centre, who placed upon his head an ornamental crown, apparently a gold one, and wore a most superb gold striped silk surplice with other finery to correspond. The other two were equally magnificent, except for their headdress, to all appearances the only distinction. Some three to four score friars[14] were seated on benches on either side of the chancel. The crowns of their heads were all shaved,[15] and a circle of black silk placed there about the size of the rim if a large tea cup; and all wore surplices.

There are great numbers of friars and priests in this superstitious country, supported by property belonging to the church, and an immense amount of land in Portugal is appropriated to that end. No preaching took place, but an abundance of bends, bows, and different motions and gestures, and a great deal of pointing with their fingers at their foreheads, cheeks, noses, chins, breasts and stomachs, each motion being proper when commemorating some particular saint. Burning incense is a custom they practised extensively: and the friars occasional intoned. I remained there for about half an hour, when the three priests began to descend the middle aisle, an elegant silk canopy being held over the central one, preceded by an elderly person dressed in a scarlet robe, and holding a long staff topped by an ornamental gilt crown; then came the friars (each carrying a lighted wax candle, about 4 feet in length and 2 or 3 inches in thickness); and the congregation followed in their wake. This procession moved out of the chapel and solemnly proceeded along several streets, the laity participating

---

14   As Bakewell termed all religious.
15   It would appear that Bakewell had never seen a tonsured head before, or perhaps knew not the word.

in the friars' singing,[16] or at least those having that gift. On their approach, the citizens instantly fell on their knees, and remained thus until the retinue had passed, all business giving way to this ceremonious rite, no matter how occupied or in what hurry they might have been; and those of the gentry in their carriages immediately stopped and alighting, fell on their knees likewise, or went through the ceremony within their vehicles. The moment this mass of superstition re-passed, *en route* to their church, everyone rose to their feet to continue their interrupted occupations.[17]

The detachment I commanded consisted of forty men belonging to the 7th, 40th, 61st, and the Brunswick Corps.[18] By the 25th, they were ready to set off towards the Lines — a three-day march.[19] I was somewhat surprised that I had been selected for this task, not knowing a word of Portuguese, nor acquainted with an inch of the road. I choose a man from the

---

16   Bakewell's described them as 'pouring forth their harmonious ejaculations'!
17   Several narratives refer to this practice, as in that by Private Wheeler, who remarked: 'There is nothing so degrading to human nature as the conduct of the people on these occasions.'
18   Eight companies of Brunswick Oels Light Infantry riflemen, or *Jägers*, had only recently arrived in the Peninsula.
19   The Lines, or rather the 'Lines of Torres Vedras' (taking its name from a village near the north-western end of the outer line) were two extensive and roughly parallel ranges of defensive fortifications constructed during the previous year by local peasant labour and the Lisbon militia under the supervision of British officers. They ran across the intricate terrain of the peninsula between the Atlantic and the Tagus at some twenty and thirty miles north of Lisbon, and were referred to by Oman as 'a ganglion of mountains rather than a well-marked chain.' Its construction had been a well-kept secret and, on reaching them unexpectedly, Masséna, who expected a walk-over, was thoroughly frustrated, realising that it would be virtually impossible to break through.

40th Regiment as my servant, who was a tolerable interpreter; and bought an ass, on which I loaded a valise I had purchased, containing a few shirts and other necessaries, leaving the rest of my clothes in a chest aboard a store vessel.

CHAPTER 3

To the Lines of Torres Vedras

WE QUIT BELÉM AT ABOUT 10 o'clock and, after traversing Lisbon, reached a village called Lumiar by evening. I had rarely seen anywhere more crowded with military than this. Just after my arrival, the great Spanish general Romana had arrived there with four thousand troops:[1] with this addition to those already installed there, I could scarcely get any cover for my convalescents: had they not just come out of the hospital, I would have encamped them in the fields; however, with making applications and searching for two hours or more, at about 11.0 I found an old barn a mile or so out of the town in which to accommodate them. I then went with my servant to a house selling bread, and never did I see more scrambling for it; and it was only with difficulty that I obtained two loaves, for which

---

1   Pedro La Romana, Marques (1761–1811), Much later, when discussing the incompetence of most Spanish generals, Wellington remarked that he 'was the worst of all – a good man – a very good excellent man, but no general'. He had been in Denmark formerly, commanding a force of 9,000 Spaniards occupying the country as an ally of the French; but in August 1808 he and his army had then been spirited away by the Royal Navy under Admiral Sir Richard Keats (1757–1834) and brought back to the Peninsula to fight them, largely in Galicia, and during Moore's campaign. He later joined Wellington behind the Lines. He died suddenly, and in Wellington's presence – probably from a heart attack – at Cartaxo on 23 January, despite the current rumour that he was poisoned, as mentioned by Bakewell.

I paid a whole dollar.[2] At this, they found space for me in one corner of a passage, where I slept on the ground wrapped in my boat cloak, while my servant lay across the passage between me and the door, so that no one could reach me without tumbling over him.

At dawn, we followed the road through Loures, that evening reaching Cabeça de Montachique, where I obtained good quarters for my detachment, and was invited to dine with the commandant, who provided a plentiful repast, Portuguese wine, and afterwards a good bed.[3] On Sunday, we continued our route, traversing Cavaleiros and Póvoa, and by 2.0 had reached the Lines at Patameira, where the 27th was stationed,[4] and received instructions to distribute my men among their respective regiments.

That task accomplished, I returned to my own regiment and was invited with two other officers to dine with the colonel commanding, Sir John Maclean at his billet;[5] but such accommodation for a colonel I did not expect to see, for our calf house [at Castle Donington], when cleaned out, is a palace in comparison. His dining table consisted of two planks or boards covered with a cloth, but upon this he had a good

2 The author added the footnote: 'When I gave a dollar for the two loaves, a voice from the crowd exclaimed: "My God, Bakewell, you are a Gentleman."'

3 Bakewell adds: 'This bed was placed on a gallery, similar to those in churches, and the servant attempted to throw me over the front, but failed for want of strength: he was tipsy.'

4 This hamlet stood behind the northerly of the two main Lines of Torres Vedras, north-east of Wellington's H.Q. at Pero Negro, and west of Sobral de Monte Agraço.

5 Lieutenant Colonel John Maclean had served in the Irish Rebellion in 1798, and commanded the 3/27th from 1808 to 1814. He was wounded at Badajoz and Toulouse. By 1838 he had become a Lieutenant General. He died in 1848.

dinner set, and gave us plenty of wine. In one corner of this
pigsty was a mattress, on which he slept. At about 11 o'clock
we retired to our quarters, mine being that of the officers of
the 2nd company.

This was my first day with the 3rd Battalion of the 27th
Regiment, which happened to coincide with Wake Sunday
at Castle Donington, where I first saw the light. I found my
bedchamber to be a barn in which most of officers dossed down
on the ground, their bedclothes being merely a boat cloak and
blanket, in which muffled state we lay beside each other, our
heads towards the wall and heels towards the centre. I slept
tolerable well considering, but the others thought themselves
fortunate to find any building in which to creep.

We noticed several bullocks approaching us next morning,
apparently from the enemy lines: nine of them strayed
through the centre of our regiment. Frederick Harding and
I,[6] with two or three others, took our men's muskets and
cartouche boxes, and pursued the herd across open country
for at least three miles, when, after repeatedly firing at them,
eight bite the dust: indeed a providential supplement to our
rations. Our regimental butchers, who soon cut them up for
us, claimed their hearts for the trouble, which together with
the kidneys, and tongues, are always allowed them, though
they generally crib a little more The officers selected some
of the best cuts and gave the men the rest, so we had plenty
of beef steaks. The following week, an officer with a flag of
truce came to claim their restoration, at which request the
Field Officer commanding the Light Brigade in advance,
returned one quarter of one of these beasts, together with a
few bottles of spirits, telling the Frenchman that they were
all cut up and largely consumed, but hoped he would accept

---

6   Frederick Harding was killed at the storming of San Sebastian.

the part sent back, on the receipt of which he was observed to doff his hat and retire.

The French lines were clearly seen from ours (the distance between us being about three miles), as we were stationed upon two opposite hills, with the French to the east of us; and at times, with our telescopes, we could plainly pick out Masséna riding up and down their lines.[7]

Our Light Brigades were within one mile of theirs, and our sentinels within gunshot, but such was the disposition of the contending powers that if you had been there you might have seen the French and the English intermixed in the vineyards as unconcerned as if they had not the least expectation of any future contests.[8] However, this only happened during a

---

7   André Masséna, Duc de Rivoli (1756–1817), and later Prince of Essling, had been a general since 1793; and had been one of Napoleon's most successful marshals until, in Wellington, meeting his match both at Busaco and Fuentes de Oñoro, at which, after his frustration at the Lines of Torres Vedras, his inglorious campaign in the Peninsula came to an end, and he was retired.

8   However much Wellington discouraged such fraternisation, it was difficult to enforce. One mid December day, French officers had approached the British. William Tomkinson (16th Light Dragoons) described the incident: they, 'having taken off their swords . . . came down to speak to us, saying their object was only foraging, and that we need not put ourselves to any inconvenience, as they should soon withdraw . . . They invited us to a play at Santarem they had got up, and we them to horse-races, football, and dog-hunts. The communication was put a stop to by a general order.' Rifleman Edward Costello likewise refers to such fraternization, remarking that they frequently met the French 'bathing in the Rio Maior, and would often have swimming and jumping matches. In these games we mostly beat them,' and that, touched with pity at their distressed and half-starved condition, our men shared with them the ration biscuits. 'Tobacco was in great request. We used to carry some of ours to them, while they in return would bring us a little brandy.'

few of the winter months, as the weather from November to March was generally very wet: the countryside during a greater part of that time was often inundated and quite impassable; but in March it usually brightens up, and seldom rains; indeed frequently not at all during the whole summer – that is until November – and when it pours in torrents, not as a drizzle as so often in England in that dismal misty way. I was told that during the previous summer they had only one shower – or, more properly, a storm – and that lasted barely half an hour; so we may reckon to have plenty of dust during the dog days.

*

At this point, Bakewell listed the names of the officers he found attached to the 3rd Battalion of the 27th Regiment, under Major General Sir Lowry Cole (also commanding the 4th Division),[9] including those setting out from Ireland with him, and attached to the regiment from 28 October to 3 November.

*

There were *Lieutenant Colonel* Sir John McLean commanding the regiment; *Majors* [William Howe] Erskine,[10] [John] Birmingham,[11] and [Peter] Nicholson; *Captains* [John R.] Ward,[12]

---

9   Sir Galbraith Lowry Cole (1772–1842) was the younger son of the first Earl of Enniskillen. He was a Cornet in 1787; a Major in 1793; a Lieutenant Colonel in 1804 and fought at Maida; a Major General and Commander of the 4th Division from 1809 to 1814; and Lieutenant General in June 1813. He commanded the 6th Division in the Waterloo Campaign, but missed the actual battle as he was getting married. From 1828 to 1838 he was Governor of the Cape of Good Hope.

10   Wounded at Badajoz 6 April 1812.

11   Died of wounds at Badajoz 11 May 1811.

12   Wounded at Badajoz.6 April 1812.

[Dawson] Kelly, [Archibald] Mair; [Thomas] White,[13] [John] Smith,[14] [Edward John] Elliot, and [John] Pring;[15] *Lieutenants* [Francis] Simcoe,[16] [Charles] Levinge,[17] [George] Lennon, [William] Dobbin,[18] [Thomas] Radcliffe,[19] [Samuel] Mangin, [Michael] White,[20] [Alexis] Thompson,[21] [William] McLean, [Charles] Crawford,[22] [James] Davidson,[23] [Thomas] Moore,[24] [Thomas] Craddock, and [John] Atkinson; *Ensigns* [Carlisle] Pollock,[25] [William] Boyle,[26] [William] Weir,[27] [Joseph] Hill,[28] [Robert Jocelyn] Phillips,[29] [James] Graham, [Frederick]

---

13 Possibly John White, who died at Torres Vedras in March 1811.

14 Killed at Badajoz 10 May 1811.

15 Wounded at Badajoz 10 May 1811.

16 Killed at Badajoz 6 April 1812.

17 Wounded at Badajoz 10 May 1811; killed there 6 April 1812.

18 Wounded at Badajoz in May 1811, and 6 April 1812.

19 Wounded at Sorauren 28 July 1813.

20 Killed at Badajoz 6 April 1812.

21 Wounded at Badajoz 6 April 1812; killed at Salamanca.

22 Died of wounds in Pyrenees 27 July 1813.

23 Wounded at Badajoz 6 April 1812; killed at Salamanca 18 July 1812

24 Wounded at Badajoz 6 April 1812.

25 Wounded at Sorauren 28 July 1813.

26 Wounded at Badajoz 10 May 1811, and Sorauren 28 July 1813.

27 In a footnote, Bakewell had commented: 'A few days after I had joined, Weare [*sic*] asked me to accompany him to the front of our advanced lines. I did not hesitate to go, but we then found ourselves accidentally in the rear of the French advanced picket. On realising this, we withdrew as fast as our heels could carry us, and I was surprised to find that the French did not fire upon us on our return . . .' Weir was wounded at Badajoz 6 April 1812 and Vitoria 21 June 1813.

28 Wounded at Vitoria 21 June 1813.

29 Wounded at Badajoz 6 April 1812.

Harding,[30] [John] Pike, [Hugh] Gough,[31] [Featherstone] Hanby,[32] [William] Sampson, [John] Mclean, and [James] McCoard.[33]

Paymaster Samuel Franklin; *Surgeon* [John] Clarke;[34] and *Assistant Surgeon* [William] Brock,[35] and H[enry] Franklin; and *Quartermaster* [Philip] Gordon.

I had not much to do at this time apart from attending parades and dining with the different officers of the regiment. Although opportunities for military advancement now lay open before me, I was more preoccupied by the danger of contracting some physical illness than being hit by a French bullet. I was soon aware that many in our medical department were dispatching men whose patriotic and courageous conduct had caused them to seek the assistance of these devils of doctors. Indeed, many returned with a just a scratch from the battlefield after having thrashed the enemy, only to be finished off by these characters.[36] They are a great evil at any time and, although in

---

30 Killed at San Sebastian 31 August 1813.

31 Killed at Toulouse 10 April 1814.

32 Wounded at Badajoz 10 May 1810, and 6 April 1812; and at Sorauren 28 July 1813.

33 See Chapter 2, footnote 6.

34 Died in Lisbon on 13 August 1811.

35 Died in Lisbon on 5 October 1811.

36 Bakewell was not alone in making such comments. John Aitchison, when an ensign in the 3rd Foot Guards, had commented that there were 'men in charge of sick now who till they came here never prescribed in their lives, and there are others who have had no practice beyond answering a prescription in an apothecary shop in England. Such men are entrusted with the lives of soldiers, but it must always be the case in a great degree while the pay remains so small as to induce those only to enter the service who would starve at home. I have myself heard a surgeon way that he had no doubt that two-thirds

the present circumstances we cannot do without them, I wish some clever and able character would publish a medical treatise – even an abridged one – describing what is applicable in some of the more general cases, that would enable one to do without the profession, and give each of us sufficient knowledge to act as our own physicians. While it may be true that a patient will know his state of health when first seeing his doctor, but he can never know how he is to finish. I have been fortunate in that I rarely had any reason to recourse to what I call 'a necessary evil', except now and then when needing a trifling boost after some disorder due to my own folly. There are only two types that ever gave me the least causes for alarm, both professional: doctors and lawyers are much to be dreaded, and require great caution if tampered with.

At 5.0 on Sunday morning, 3 November, our regiment was ordered to take the field in company with the rest of the Division. This consisted of three brigades: the right being the 27th, 97th, and 40th; the centre brigade was formed by the 1st Battalion of the Portuguese Lusitanians,[37] and the 11th and the 23rd regiments (Portuguese); while the Light Brigade contained three fusilier battalions: two of the 7th Foot, and one of the 23rd Welch.

We were ordered to parade upon an adjacent hill, close to the general's billet, about two miles from our lines, to witness the execution of Private James Mulligan of the 27th, sentenced to be shot for desertion and attempting to join the enemy. The culprit, under escort, and dressed in white from head to foot,

---

of the deaths in this army were due to the inattention and ignorance of the medical officers.'

37   Members of the independently formed Loyal Lusitanian Legion, commanded by Colonel Sir Robert Wilson (1777–1849); it was disbanded in May 1811 and reformed as the 7th and 8th *Caçadores*.

now approached us, on ground set as a square, the Division forming three side of it. After the solemn procession had marched in slow time along the whole line, Mulligan was left standing in the centre on a pile of earth already dug from his grave. When a priest approached to ask whether he had anything to say that might mitigate his punishment, he answered in the negative. The guard of a dozen or so rank and file then marched twenty paces in front of him and, at the drop of a white handkerchief, discharged a volley. As their muskets had been charged with bolt, his body was mangled in a most shocking manner, one part falling into the grave. Before returning to quarters, the Division was then deliberately marched past the corpse to let each soldier see the awful spectacle, which should have been sufficient deterrent to any other prospective deserters.

The officers of the 2nd company, to which I was attached, together with those of the 1st and Grenadiers, were billeted in a barn well provided with furniture taken from the dwelling of those peasants who had abandoned this part of the country. Our Light Company was with the Light Brigade about half a mile in advance of us, and the other six companies were at least a mile to our rear. We generally rose at 3.0 in the morning, formed ourselves behind a hill, and remained there till daylight (which was at about 6.0), as it was expected that the French might well attack; and I suppose – by that hour – the whole of our line was formed, though irregularly, as my Lord Wellington, attended by his staff, used to pass by us every morning before daylight, usually between 4 and 5 o'clock.

On Sunday mornings, the Protestant prayers were read at the drum head by the Revd George Jenkins, our divisional chaplain, though they were very much abridged; and occasionally he ended by given us a sermon, but not a very long one: usually of ten minutes duration.

CHAPTER 4

Interlude at Mafra

LORD WELLINGTON SENT A NOTICE to all commissioned officers in the British, Portuguese and Spanish service under his command, to acquaint them that General William Carr Beresford would be invested with the honour of knighthood on Tuesday 27 November 1810 at the Palace of Mafra.[1] This was a country residence of the Portuguese kings, situated about thirty miles from Lisbon. Although a high proportion of these officers were invited to dine with him that day and to witness the investiture, one field officer from each brigade would have to remain at the Lines, and two commissioned officers with each company or troop, just in case the enemy choose to make a move precisely at that time.

Early on that Tuesday morning, Lieutenant Francis Simcoe called to ask whether I would accompany him to the event, also offering me his mule, an invitation I did not hesitate to accept.[2]

---

1   William, Viscount Beresford (1768–1854), an illegitimate son of the Marquess of Waterford, had served in several fields; and after a term as Military Commandant at Lisbon, had been created a Marshal of the Portuguese army, and had done sterling work in training and instilling discipline in their troops.

2   Bakewell later commented that Simcoe, the only son surviving of John Graves Simcoe (1752–1806), commander of the Queen's Rangers during the American War of Independence, and a lieutenant-general from October 1798, was in expectation of estates to the value of from between £4,000 and £5,000 per annum in the following year. The Earl of Moira was his guardian,

At 8.0 I mounted the beast, equipped in the Portuguese fashion, and we rode across country for nearly four leagues, a greater part of the way being over uneven hills and into rugged vales; but my mule climbed like a cat, and it took barely three hours to reach Mafra from Patameira.

This palace was indeed a magnificent structure,[3] far more extensive than I had yet seen in this country, or elsewhere. It is built in the form of a square, each side being nearly of equal length as the front, which I paced. At about midday, Captain [John] Smith, Simcoe and I, and several other officers from different regiments, entered the adjacent village to have lunch, as we did not expect to dine before 6 o'clock at the earliest. Here we found very good house, but so crowded with rank and distinguished characters that we had great difficulty in obtaining any food; but at length – our patience almost exhausted – we were served some cold chicken and good wine. After our collation we returned to the palace, where we had some fifteen steps to climb to reach the grand entrance.

---

but Francis Simcoe 'was unfortunately popped off at Badajoz' [this was on 6 April 1812] only a few month prior to reaching his majority. He added that 'a more honourable character never wore a red coat, and on my first introduction on the Peninsula I received great kindness and hospitality from him.'

3   The immense quadrangle, its west front some 220 metres long, being part palace and part convent, was erected by Dom João V from 1717. The church was consecrated in 1730, and the whole within the next five years; but the cost hastened the financial ruin of the country despite the riches of Brazil flooding in. In 1808, after Junot's defeat, it briefly accommodated seven British regiments at once. Robert Southey reported that the friar who accompanied him round the Library had suggested that 'it would make an excellent room to eat and drink in', while when Byron visited the monastery in 1809 – in his opinion an example of 'magnificence without elegance' – the monks had asked him 'if the English had any books in their country?'

It was on these that I first caught sight of our General by day. I might have seen him before when passing along our lines at dusk or dawn, but not knowing exactly how he looked I may not have recognised him. Lady Emily Berkeley hung on his arm.[4]

Folding doors opened into the main hall, in which stood a great number of large busts at equal distance from each other. On advancing further into the building, we entered one if the most tasteful and well-proportioned churches I ever saw, at the far end of which was a priest performing some ceremony. High up near the vaulting, and embellished with carved and gilt figures, were eight individual organs, which, being all playing together, reverberated with a grand sound. Dispersed throughout the conventual dependencies of the great building were a variety of statues portraying Faith, Hope, Charity, Peace, Plenty, the Virgin Mary, etc., interspersed by valuable old paintings depicting famous Portuguese, distinguished either in government, in war, or by their pen during the period when the country was in a prosperous state, and with a commanding presence in the world. The tables, walls, floors and ceilings, and the numerous huge pillars – apparently of solid marble – added immensely to the magnificence of the edifice.

We continued our perambulations, and came across so many rooms, chambers, etc. of all shapes and sizes that it would take too much space to particularise them here. We then ascended to the top of the building, where we found an extensive ring of bells, and a set of musical chimes, which plays for five minutes every quarter of an hour. Indeed, these chimes, which perform

---

4   This was Emilia Charlotte Berkeley (1762–1832), daughter of General Lord George Lennox and wife of Vice-Admiral Sir George Cranfield Berkeley (1753–1818), then in command of the Portuguese station.

a number of different tunes, are considered a great curiosity.[5] Next to me, accompanied by several Spanish nobles, stood a jolly robust gentleman who was very minutely observing these melodious instruments, and when I asked Simcoe if he knew who he was, he replied that it was the respected and popular General Romana.

While descending, we were told that Lord Wellington was shortly to perform the ceremony of investiture in a large and commodious room adjoining the dining ones, as being better adapted for the purpose. We repaired there to find several hundred officers already crowded in to witness the event; indeed, so many that I could scarcely obtain a glimpse of the object of our attention; and as the ceremony lasted no longer than fifteen minutes, I could hardly describe it as from my personal observation, so great was the crush.[6] After it was over, a welcome messenger arrived to say that dinner was ready in a suit of rooms along the front of the palace.

I joined the throng, and by chance found a seat in the second room of perhaps between a dozen and a score, of equal size and in a direct line from one end of this mansion to the other. Each was provided with a brace of blazing chandeliers above every set of tables, all most elegantly adorned with pieces

---

5   The carillon had been cast at Malines, near Brussels, in 1730.

6   The Hon. Sir Charles Colville (1770–1843), who had landed at Lisbon a month earlier to command a brigade in General Picton's 3rd Division, and later commanded the 3rd Division at the Nivelle, was not so easily impressed, remarking that 'The ceremony itself was far from grand or imposing, consisting of nothing more than the reading (inarticulate enough) of two short papers by his Lordship, and his laying his sword on the new Knight's shoulder,' after which, apparently it was noticed that Wellington had some difficulty in replacing it in its scabbard. Colville was served eventually with 'a plate of pigs' head stewed and some half raw ham,' which, with some sweet biscuits, made his dinner.

of cut glass, while the service was all of solid silver. When the doors were flung open – or rather when the partitions between each room were slid back into a kind of casement – these divisions disappeared at the same moment, causing such a blaze of light over the brilliant multitude that it quite stunned us. Seven to eight hundred officers, resplendent in their uniforms, displaying their medals, their stars and orders, and decorated with diamonds and other jewellery, provided one of the grandest sights I had ever seen. However, I soon picked out my Lord our Commander, as the alignment of the tables gave each individual an admirable view of the whole.

The dinner consisted of every delicacy that could be procured. A variety of fish, flesh and fowl, was followed by a plentiful dessert of fruits and sweetmeats, for the abundance of which this country has every reason to boast, particularly the former – and a great assortment of wines. John Ward of the 27th observed that if the waiters should not happen to be regular in their attendance, he would show me where I might help myself;[7] and taking me to and opening a pair of folding doors close by, we found ourselves in a room as large as a small church, in which bottles were placed two deep on the floor, as tightly packed as they could be, and to which many of the officers went to help themselves.

But a whisper now went round that a ball was about to commence in an adjoining room: those gentlemen who wanted to dance had better look fast, as there were few enough ladies available: perhaps thirty in all. I left my seat for the ballroom at about 9 o'clock, where I noticed my Lord

---

7   Captain John R. Ward, later attached as Major to the 7th Portuguese *Caçadores*, was severely wounded at Badajoz in 1812; and when gazetted Brevet Lieutenant Colonel, he commanded them at Salamanca.

Wellington leading down Lady Emily Berkeley, followed by my Lord Clinton,[8] the new made Knight, the Spanish and the Portuguese nobles, et al.

As there was a Portuguese lady from Lisbon looking on, in conversation with whom I supposed to be her mother, I asked her to be my partner; but she, not speaking English, answered: '*No comprehenda Signior*'; but when I put on my gloves, and shuffled my feet, then said: '*Si Signior, comprehenda*'. I danced with her the whole evening as they did not change every so often, as is the custom in England, but although there was little enough to be learned from our conversation, she was a good partner, and understanding some of her movement, I spent a very pleasant evening in her company. This continued until 1 o'clock, when we were informed that supper was ready. Having taken some refreshment, I bade farewell to my partner, and went to look for Simcoe, who I soon found and, after quaffing a few more glasses of wine, together with several officers of the 40th and 97th, we left the palace as the clock struck 3.0.

We had not ridden far when, hearing the noise of waves, it became obvious that we were going towards the sea by mistake.[9] Although numerous stars were glistering, it was very dark; but our real excuse for having taken the wrong road was the amount we had drunk. However, we wheeled round to find ourselves facing the palace gates again just as it was striking 4.0. A second attempt was made in a different direction, but after three or four miles we seemed to be hemmed in by stone walls; and as the others did not want to turn back, we all dismounted, tethered our mounts to some olive trees, and slept

---

8   Major General Sir Henry Clinton (1771–1829), commanding the 6th Division.

9   Mafra lies some six miles from the coast.

on the ground beside them. I preferred to lean against a tree, bridle in hand, until light appeared, when I awoke them, and we soon saw what had happened.[10]

By following yet another route, we regained Patameira between 9.0 and 10.0 o'clock. Exhausted, I repaired to our new hut, for the fatigue parties of the regiment had erected a few for the officers' to shelter them during the rainy season, tents not being permitted, due to the difficulty if transporting them. However, only a few huts had been erected before we were ordered to move from lower Patameira to what is called the upper town.[11]

10　The party had inadvertently entered the extensive walled park east of the palace.

11　From Patameira de Baixo to Patameira de Cima.

CHAPTER 5

Sitting it Out

WE REMAINED HERE [PATAMEIRA] ONLY a few days, for on 15 November we were told that Masséna had commenced his retreat with the whole French army, leaving behind part of his artillery; and our orders were to follow with all possible dispatch. Many officers were surprised to learn of Masséna's move, apparently without any cause; and a rumour spread that he had been tempted and bought by English guineas, which many thought possible.

On the first day's pursuit, we traversed Sobral [de Monte Agraço], to find it completely stripped by the French: houses burnt, and churches defiled, having been used as necessaries, and left full of shit.[1] That night, our brigade slept at Freira; and next day advanced three leagues further via Vila Nova [da Rainha] to Alenquer; and on the following night reached Azambuja, a tough four-league march through pouring rain: we seemed to have had a ten to fifteen-minute storm every half hour, and were frequently up to our middles in water, the roads well nigh impassable due to deep flooding. The 4th Division took up their quarters at Azambuja and Virtudos; and as the French had come to a full stop at Santarém, our General fixed his headquarters at Cartaxo, while the other division [? perhaps referring to the 5th] also took up a position nearby.

---

1   As Bakewell noted, 'The front of the galleries furnished them with seats.'

The countryside through which we passed was totally uninhabited: every house plundered, and many burnt out. Our officers occupied a large one at the upper end of Azambuja, which we found quite bare.[2] A boat-cloak and blanket was our bed, and a few canteens were our utensils.

As every officer is allowed a horse – though some kept two – I bought a Spanish one, its mane and tail forming a conspicuous part,[3] for 70 dollars. They were largely employed to carrying our clothing, etc., and to ride when not on the march. When turned into fields for fodder, there was great agitation amongst them, being stallions, for they are not gelded here.

Azambuja is only a mile or so north of the Tagus, by which supplies reached us by boat from Lisbon, which was a great advantage, although the natives had also established a market, which answered well while we here. Our General issued orders that every soldier who molested or defrauded any of those bringing in provisions would be punished with the greatest severity, and a few examples were made. Some privates who had eased a baker of his load without making any compensation got flogged to a degree almost past bearing. This gave the

---

2   The construction of the Lines of Torres Vedras was an obvious and vital element of Wellington's scheme for the defence of Lisbon. Almost as important was the implementation and stringent enforcement of his 'scorched earth' policy, which would deny the French all sustenance, for meanwhile the civilian population of the hinterland had been instructed to retire behind the Lines together with their livestock. While this caused them very considerable hardship, it eventually forced the French, isolated and unable to subsist, and with the prospect of impending starvation, to retreat, leaving wide swathes of destruction and desolation in their wake.

3   The British cavalry 'nag-tailed' or docked their mounts, which also served to distinguish them at a distance from the un-docked French. Whether officers' personal horses were similarly treated is questionable.

peasantry greater confidence in our punctuality in paying, which lead them to keep us well and regularly supplied.

The riverside meadows were excellent pasturage, but the soil further from the Tagus became gradually more sandy and dry, and was planted with orange and lemon groves, fig trees, almonds, and plums, etc., although vineyards predominated. There were also numerous olive-groves, providing the peasantry with the oil they live on, and to which they are very partial, adding it to their salads and almost everything else they eat. They are also fond of puddings; have plenty of rice, milk, and fruit in profusion; and their wines are excellent.

The inhabitants, who had deserted the district on the appearance of the French, had not yet returned to it, and we found any amount of furniture, provisions, etc. hidden in their homes, fields, and gardens. The first step taken by our troops on entering a house bearing any appearance of prosperity, was to ransack every corner, pulling up the floor-boards to find plate, watches, and other valuables possibly concealed there, as thought to be a secure place; and we extracted pewter dishes, pieces of furniture, etc., buried four or five feet in the ground. We discovered a quantity of salt pork, etc., secreted in a well, over which a board had been placed and then covered with earth; and in one church we came across a collection of fancy surplices in a large chest of drawers. These had not been hidden, on the assumption that, belonging to the Church, they would be respected; but they shared the same fate as the rest of any property found, and came in useful as night-gowns or cloaks. Many of the convents were attached to churches, but both were soon converted into barracks and crammed with troops.

As the duration our stay here was uncertain, the 27th did not form a mess (as their plate had remained in Lisbon), so we dined together by detachments in our respective cells, each quartering four officers; but in the evenings, although we often had a general muster, grog and wine flowed; many a song was sung, and a merry time was spent together.

The fish, fruits, vegetables, etc. brought to us from Lisbon, were usually sold to us at the following prices:

Fish, 2 *vints* per lb;[4] butter and cheese, 24 *vints* per lb; a brace of fowl or duck, 3½ and 4 dollars respectively; pigeons, 1 dollar each; tea, 3 dollars per lb; for both figs and grapes, 3 *vints* per lb; oranges and lemons, 4 and 5 for 1 *vint*: of which they appear always to be plenty, as one crop frequently hangs on the tree till the succeeding one becomes ripe; potatoes, 4 *vints* per lb (but these are imported from Ireland); melons, 3 and 4 *vints* each; port and white wine, 8 and 10 *vints* per quart; brandy and rum, 5 dollars per quart; a Portuguese spirit called 'acquident' [*aguardente*] (something like our gin, but not so clear), 2 dollars per quart; ale and porter imported from England from 24 to 30 *vints* per quart; beef, pork, veal, mutton, etc. was not to be bought at any price. I had only once seen a butcher since my arrival in this country, and that was in Lisbon: we received meat only at our cantonments.

The officers amuse themselves in shooting, coursing, foot-racing, and playing cricket, etc.; and on every Tuesday evening a meeting took place, conducted by a committee of three, with the object of issuing a weekly paper, to which it was expected that every one holding a commission would contribute a specimen of his literary prowess: when published, it was called the 'Virtudos Gazette', as our meetings took place in that village.

Football was much played. Captain Smith, who commanded the Grenadier Company, challenged other captains in the Regiment that twenty of his men would play the best of three games with twenty chosen men from any other company,

---

4   40 *vints* made one dollar, which was valued at 5/-.

for a bet of 100 dollars, which Captain John Pring,[5] who commanded the Light Company, accepted. As there were no fences in this country, the terrain presented a fine playing-field for the sport. Two poles, about 6 feet in length, were placed about two yards apart at each end of the field, which was about one mile in length. A ball was thrown up in the centre; and the contending parties had to kick it between one of the goals before either could claim to win the game. The 5ft 8-inch men were too fast for the 6 ft ones, but although there was only one hole in the ground, one or more of these taller men always managed to trip and fall into it. The two games were won with ease by the Light Company, and in half an hour only, to the no little disappointment of our Grenadier Captain. These two companies then united, with forty men proposing to play forty of any selected from the remaining eight companies. This was accepted by the battalion companies, and a great game it was, but neither side could claim the victory: after playing for two days, twelve hours each day, both sides gave it up, neither of them able to kick the ball between the poles . . . so they agreed to a draw.

Horse-racing was another amusement. On one occasion I entered my mount, rode it in a two-mile heat, and came second. As hares proliferated here, and the officers were well provided with greyhounds, they frequently went coursing. Cricket was played two or three times each week, the Revd George Jenkins being very partial to the game, and was considered one of the best battmen [sic] in the Division. Later on, in January, Lord Wellington sent to message to us that he would soon require our assistance to play with different kinds of balls than cricket ones.

On 3 December the 27th Regiment was ordered to proceed from Azambuja to Virtudos, one league further up country.

---

5   He was to be severely wounded at Badajoz on 10 May 1811.

This was a miserable village containing from seventy to eighty dwellings or – more properly – huts or hovels, being one storey high only and without doors or windows, as the former, together with almost all the furniture, had been used to kindle fires by the French on their retreat; and thus – as it was in the depth of what little winter they have here – our slumbers were cold ones; though, apart from one morning, I never saw any appearance of frost throughout the whole winter, nor ice on the water, but the ground was white and tinselled over with a kind of heavy dew. However, we had frequent cold and heavy showers, and as our habitations were scarcely water-proof, we had great difficulty in finding a dry spot. But the officers requisitioned what they termed fatigue parties, and with the help of a few masons, soon sheltered themselves from the rain; and we got some chimneys built, and fire-places on one corner of our dwellings, for the Portuguese had no such things. What little fire they used was made of charcoal placed in a small square grate – removable at pleasure, as it was not a fixture – and on this the Portuguese boiled their water, their vegetables and what little meat they could find, as 1 lb of veal, mutton, or beef would be as much as they were able to place upon the table for a family of ten or a dozen; a large joint is never seen except among the first and most distinguished company.

The local inhabitants brought us little in the way of provisions during our time at Virtudos, but our Commissary was very regular in distributing our daily rations. Each man should receive 1 lb of either beef, pork, or mutton; 1½ lbs of bread, and 1 pint of wine, from the colonel down to the private; but I could never understand why the commissioned officers were charged only 3d per day for them, and all the others charged 6d.

However rough our quarters, we spent many a pleasant hour here. At 8.0 on 18 January 1811 our battalion was ordered to repair to Azambuja, as a certain Matthew Poirs had been caught in the act of desertion, an unpardonable offence, for which there was no mitigation, the culprits being always either shot or hanged, the latter fate being decreed in his case. The whole Division, consisting of nine battalions (whose strength in the field was 8,000 men), assembled in a square a mile from the town; and at about 10 o'clock Poirs made his appearance, escorted by a strong guard. After tying his legs together and pinioning him, he was hung on a large tree in the centre of the square, where he departed in a few minutes without a struggle.

At 2.0 next morning we received unexpected orders to be in readiness to march at 5.0, which put us all in a bustle and confusion, but at the appointed hour we were all formed up with our baggage paraded, waiting for instructions as to what route to take. However, at 11.0 the order was countermanded: no march would take place, so we were dismissed and repaired to our former quarters. But we did not stay there long, for on 25 January we were ordered back to Azambuja, as our battalion, being three miles in advance, was not considered safe, for the French in our front and towards Santarém had become very restive.

It was from this date on that the light troops of both armies were to be seen skirmishing daily, and it was at this period that General Junot – commonly called the Duke of Abrantes – received a slap in the face, a private of the 16th Light Dragoons having shot away part of his nose.[6] It was on 29 January that we heard of the sudden death of General Romana.

---

6   Andoche Junot, Duc d'Abrantes (1771–1813), who had commanded the first French invasion of Portugal in 1807, was defeated by Wellington (then still known as Wellesley) at the battle of Vimeiro on 21 August 1808. It was during a skirmish at Rio Maior that a ball broke his nose and lodged in his cheek, from which it was extracted with difficulty. A member of the 1st Hussars of the KGL named Drôge, is said to have fired the shot.

On 1st February the Division was ordered to proceed five miles to witness Anthony Hasse, a private in the Brunswick Corps, shot for deserting. This crime was no means general amongst the Lines, but now and then one or more men would attempt to join the enemy, although our outlying vedettes and pickets usually picked them up on the passage.

On Friday 15 February the 3rd Battalion of the 27th; consisting of 1,100 men – with no one to be absent, except though illness – was ordered to be ready for inspection by General Cole, at which he expressed his satisfaction at the appearance of his regiment. This was followed by an order from Lord Wellington that the entire 4th Division, under Cole's command, be paraded at 10.0 on the morning of the 22nd on ground a few miles from us. His Lordship arrived at about 11.0, accompanied by his staff, etc., when the Division was first put through the manual, platoon, and the usual manoeuvres, after which he complimented us on the precision in which they had been undertaken, and observed that the Division was well disciplined. It was generally believed, that whenever an inspection by our Commander-in-Chief took place, an engagement is in contemplation. (His Lordship appears to be about the middle stature: from 5 ft 9 to 5ft 10 inches; a little corpulent,[7] and of rather fair complexion.)

That evening I went into the adjutant's billet, where, on showing me a list of the French regiments in Portugal, and giving their strength, position, etc., I asked him what numbers his Lordship had under his command with which to oppose this force. He answered and said 110,000, but not more than 35,000 of them were British; a greater number were Portuguese troops, and the rest, Spanish. I doubt whether Great Britain

---

7   This is a surprising comment, and I wonder whether Bakewell, in so-describing him, intended another word.

had ever sent abroad so many able bodied and active troops at any former period; and – as it will appear in the sequel – it was these who were obliged to bear the brunt, and did the greater part of the execution against the common enemy, and were responsible for so many victories being won.[8]

---

8   This was the view of the great majority of both the officers and the rank and file, although after the battle of Busaco they had a far better opinion of the fighting qualities of the Portuguese, once disciplined and trained, with British officers seconded to command their units, which were incorporated by then into what was an Anglo-Portuguese army. So far, the behaviour of Spanish troops – as at Talavera or Barrosa – had given their allies very little confidence in them, although it was admitted that on certain occasions, when facing the French together, as at Albuera, some Spanish units had stood their ground: but this was rare.

Although, much later in the war, some Spanish troops had fought well, when under Wellington's more direct control, but even at the combat at San Marcial (31 August 1813), when given the opportunity to show their mettle when in action unaided, and which in their account of the war was represented as one of their greatest battles – as a feat that did them the highest honour – it was hardly that. British officers who witnessed the engagement reported that as at one time so many ran away, a brigade of guards close to their position actually received orders to form a guard in order to 'stop all Spanish soldiers who were not wounded'.

CHAPTER 6

In Pursuit of Masséna

AT THIS TIME OF THE year the weather begins to clear; flooded areas were drying up and the roads becoming passable, which disposed our general to make a move. The campaign may be said to date from 5 March 1811, the day we began to act on the offensive.

By 9.0 that morning our Division was in readiness with baggage paraded. The first day's march brought us to a village called Pontével,[1] to which we found that some of the natives had already returned, and where I was to billet in a well-furnished house occupied by an old lady, the owner, and her servant; but she refused to be troubled, and said she would not take in soldiers. I, being but a young one, on applying to the proper quarter for orders, was instructed to unship the old lady; so I sent my servant, who spoke the language fluently, together with a file of men, to do that. He soon returned with the key, saying he had put them both in the street. The officers attached to the 2nd company spent the evening with me, after which we settled into two or three of the beds and slept very comfortably, and at 5 o'clock next morning we took some chocolate before setting off. On quitting our roost, the first thing we saw on opening the door was the old lady sitting on the steps, bathed in tears. I told my servant to explain to her that we had only made use of her furniture and not touched a

---

1   This stands at no great distance due west of Cartaxo.

thing, which placated her somewhat, for she had been assumed that – like the French – we would have taken half of it away and destroyed the rest. Indeed, she was so relieved that she said she would be glad to see us should we pass that way again.

Within four hours we had reached Cartaxo, our new headquarters; but as our intention was to capture Santarém (that of the French), we pressed forward rapidly, entering one side of the town as they retired from the other. We were surprised that the enemy had not resisted, for the place had not only provided them with secure cantonments, but was well situated for defence. Instead, on their departure, they did all they could to destroy anything they couldn't carry off. Its churches were most scandalously bedaubed with every kind of nastiness, and filth lay in heaps one and two feet deep in many places; houses had been set alight in several areas, and so effectively that there was scarcely a roof left on any of them: except for one, converted into a theatre, where apparently their officers had displayed their theatrical talents to full houses; and it could seat over three hundred. It had been most elegantly furnished with all that was needed: scenery, costumes, chandeliers, etc. But to do this, they had stripped fourteen convents and churches and numerous dwellings, from which they had taken whatever they wanted in the way of splendid ornaments to decorate and equip two tiers of boxes, a pit, gallery, and the stage, which they had left behind un-destroyed in their precipitate retreat. Any furniture not collected there had long been consumed.

The French had also left some of their dead unburied behind them: others, in a dying state and unable to bear the fatigue of the march, they dispatched, filling the springs and fountains with the corpses to infect our water-supplies.

The 1st, 4th, and 6th divisions were quartered in Santarém this evening, but a more desolate place I had never seen: only naked walls were left standing for our protection; but our

Commissary was very regular in the distribution of our rations whenever they could reach us: and this was essential, for we had nothing else to depend on but what they supplied.

Next morning (7 March), the three divisions left Santarém for another day's march, passing scenes I had never witnessed: dead and dying men, horses, asses and mules lay strewn along the road for five long leagues as far as Golegã, reached that evening. I was told that it was the rapidity of the British advance that caused the enemy to jettison so much lumber, among which were numerous wounded and disabled, dragged from their hospitals and just left on the roads to make their last exits; nor did we think them – even those living – a prize sufficiently valuable to pick up, as there was no danger in leaving them in our rear, even if there was not a quarter of a mile in the whole day's route clear of the dead and the dying.

And when we reached Golegã, I found it a more miserable place than Santarém, if that was possible, for the houses were entirely ransacked and plundered of everything except the vermin, and of that there was in abundance, for their walls, ceilings, and floors were covered with fleas, lice, etc. However, with difficulty, I obtained two chairs, and an old door, which I washed down and slept upon that night; but before daylight I felt something gnawing at the calf of my leg. I reached to catch it, and laid fast hold of a rat's tail! I was not sorry when the bugles sounded for our advance, which was through Atalaia, while in the evening we entered Tomar, in which and in the neighbourhood almost the whole of Lord Wellington's forces, consisting of one hundred thousand men or more,[2] were concentrated by the following morning.

---

2   At this time, according to Oman (IV, p. 134), the numbers in the three divisions concerned were: 1st: 8,000 (of all ranks, and all British); 4th: 4,800 British, and 2,100 Portuguese; and 6th: 3,850 British, and 2,300 Portuguese.

It was here that I first bumped into two of the sons of the Revd Phillip Storey of Lockington, near Donington, each commanding a troop in the 3rd Dragoon Guards, attached to our division (for each division of infantry had a brigade of artillery, and a proportionate number of cavalry acting with it.)

Tomar is rather a handsome town, with some good squares in it, and on a hill above stands an extensive convent, one side of which command a view of the whole.[3] We stayed here on the 9th, and at 6.0 next day the drums beat the march to advance. We waited, formed in line, until midday, when we were told that the 2nd Division, under the command of General Spencer,[4] had been ordered to the south for the purpose of attacking the garrisons of Campo Maior – Badajoz, etc. – while ours, the 4th, was supposed to be destined for the north with the remaining divisions, that is for Oporto, Guarda, etc.

At about noon we were ordered to proceed with all dispatch, but except a few general officers, we never knew where until the evening, when we encamped in fields belonging to the village of Sabacheira.[5] A line was fixed where the men's muskets were to be piled, and we were ordered to sleep within five paces of them. The officers were allowed to settle down

---

3   This was the impressive Convento de Cristo, largely dating from 1160 to 1600, built round its 16-sided Templar church. It is uncertain whether Bakewell was one of several officers curious enough to explore it, as did Colonel Sir Augustus Simon Frazer (Royal Horse Artillery) on his way to the front in January 1813, who found the noble convent, in which the French were formerly quartered, still 'in ruins; fine paintings on the chapel torn to pieces, and many carried away; the organ broken, the altars thrown down, fireplaces made in all the cloisters, and every thing broken and defaced . . . in wanton barbarity.'

4   General Sir Brent Spencer (1760–1828) commanded c. 6,100 of all ranks.

5   This lies about 7 miles north-west of Tomar.

further away, but still near enough to join instantly in case of surprise. Our habit was to throw a blanket over our shoulders and take our rest at the root of a tree or under some hillock that would secure us from the wind, as neither tents nor scarcely any luggage (except a change of linen) could be taken with us from this date, when we began to experience all the severities of a fatiguing campaign.

The drums beat an hour before daylight for our assembling and we had half an hour to dress and shave if necessary – this being done without a mirror and frequently without soap (there were always men with the regiment that would keep our razors in good order) – and to take our breakfast, which was usually a little hot chocolate. Should any officer – no matter what his rank, except the Officer Commanding – absent himself at this period, they would set off without him, leaving no instructions as to how he might follow.

The 4th Division left Sabacheira very early on the 11th and proceeded across country towards a village called Pombal, reached at dusk; and as we were forming our line on one side of the town we found the enemy encamped on a hill on the far side, about three miles beyond. We could plainly observe them busy around their fires, supposedly cooking their dinners. Our men piled their arms in a line, taking up positions a proper distance in the rear (the advanced vedettes and pickets being previously formed), and began to kindle our own fires and prepare our dinners, and not before time, having had a long and fatiguing march.[6]

On these occasions, it was not permitted to take more luggage than is absolutely necessary. A mule is attached to each company of 100 men, which is called the camp-kettle mule, and for every ten men it carries a frying pan and a boiling

---

6   Some 18 miles across country.

kettle made for the purpose.[7] These utensils are always with the regiment, and will cook a steak, etc. in a few minutes. After our meal we threw ourselves on the ground in the rear of the line, rolled in a blanket, not only fully dressed, but also with our accoutrements on, as ordered. At that time, we only stripped once or twice a week, and that was when we changed our linen.

Drums beat the assembly early on the 12th, and we were on the march before daylight, our Light Division, consisting of the Light Company of each regiment, collected in our rear; but when we had marched about three miles, they passed us at a jog trot with their arms trailed, and within three minutes had caught up with the enemy rearguard, when skirmishing immediately commenced, for pop-pop was the order of the day; and the rest of us followed them towards Redinha, where the French had chosen to make a stand.

On approaching it, we passed many of their wounded and dead, winged or dispatched by the bullets of our Light Division; and, on reaching a hill within one mile of Redinha, saw the French formed in lines about three-quarters of a mile in our front.[8] We halted for a few minutes, when I could plainly see that French had chosen the more advantageous ground, for the hill-slope upon which our lines were drawn up was much lower, with a valley between us. Their artillery, further uphill and in the rear of their infantry, could fire over their heads; and when our lines began to descend into the valley, their

---

7   As far as I am aware, the heavy cast-iron camp kettles then in use were not replaced by light sheet-metal ones until the following year; this would allow smaller groups to cook at short notice.

8   This would have been the division commanded by General Mermet (1772–1837), with that of General Marchand (1765–1851) behind it, forming Masséna's rearguard.

guns thundered at us in great style and did some execution, although many shells went buzzing over our heads. To avoid further casualties – inevitable if we pressed ahead – General Cole ordered us to turn to the right about face and retire behind the hill we had just left, and our artillery, which had been in our rear, was brought forward to fire on the French, who were not expecting this arm, which made great havoc and slaughter among two regiments of their cavalry which were well advanced, with the intention of attacking and cutting off our right wing. Their surviving cavalry about faced in double quick time and rapidly disappeared. Our heavy guns were then levelled at their infantry lines, and gave them such a lesson that they retreated as rapidly.

During this time, the company to which I was attached was ordered into the valley to repair a partly destroyed bridge, and I was up to the middle in water, placing stones in a way that would allow us to cross a rivulet. We now pushed directly into Redinha to find it already ablaze and the roofs of many buildings falling in, but although the adage of 'better late than never' applied, and we were there in time to save some of their furniture at least.

The place of the officers and men when making the attack was as follows: the men formed in two-deep line, the captain in the front rank to give commands when closely engaged, the colonel in the centre of the regiment, and the two majors with the respective wings. The subalterns were in the rear of their companies and, behind them, a certain number of experienced and trusty drill-sergeants. When the contending lines were within a few hundred paces of each other, the generals remained well back, out of range of musketry.

In this instance, I don't think our general and field officers would had much hope of succeeding had they persevered in the face of the French artillery, for when passing over the ground where ours had fired at the enemy cavalry, I was surprised to see the lacerating effect of these destructive machines and the slaughter they had made. I picked up one man's arm, wrenched from his shoulder, and carried it ten yards to the body it had belonged to: legs and other members lay scattered about.

We encamped that evening at Redinha.

Next morning (13 March), we were on the march as soon as it was light, while our Light Division, their arms trailed, went trotting past us as on the previous morning; but they had not gone long before the popping commenced, having again caught up with the enemy rearguard, and skirmishing and the sound of heavy musketry fire continued all day long while on our way to Condeixa, where we halted and slept in adjacent fields, the town being ablaze. Even when we were close behind them, the enemy always seemed to find time to burn and destroy. Throughout this day's march we passed a great many wounded and dead, both English and French, mostly the latter, the majority of them being 'winged', that is shot either in the legs or arms, but a good share of them were in the head or trunk, when it was usually fatal.

We quit Condeixa's fields just before daylight after securing those prisoners we had taken – including those disabled – which, during the two preceding days, amounted to a few hundred. During that morning, we found that the French had altered their route, not retreating towards Coimbra and the north, as expected, but instead, they had wheeled off to the right over a barren and deserted area, traversed by such rugged tracks that no vehicles of any description could easily follow them. I suppose this was why their artillery and commissariat, etc., when leaving Condeixa, took a different route, intending to converge later. Suffice it to say that neither could our own Commissary accompany us, and this was the first time that I remember that he, together with our division's supplies, failed to keep up.

We marched a great distance this day (eight leagues), which was very harassing and fatiguing, and after traversing a village called Espinheiro,[9] at dusk we reached the fields of Espinhal, where we bivouacked. I was the officer on the regimental guard that night, and there was no sleep for me. Although this was a bore, it turned out opportunely, for Corporal Oakes happened to go into one of the cottages to find the peasant owner taking nine loaves from his oven, which he immediately seized, although contrary to orders, but necessity pays no respect to authority. He gave me one, which was very seasonable for having had no rations we were hungry. As the poor man had no meat, no bread, no wine, no spirits, or anything else, 1½ dollars was offered for a biscuit, but he then had the cheek to ask Captain Smith two dollars for it, which was no larger than a spice-cake.

I was relieved from guard duty at 8.0, but as there was neither Commissary nor provisions yet at hand, we could not pursue the enemy without at least the prospect of supplies, as there was nothing other than olive trees and a few unfenced bean fields in this open countryside. Nor stone walls: they make a small ditch round each field, and place a stone at each corner, that each may distinguish his own property and produce. Most of road along which we trudged the previous day passed through nothing except gorse and other prickly shrubs. However, our men climbed into the olive trees to eat until they were as black as a bilberry. It is from these that the peasants extract their oil. I tasted but did not relish the olives at all. The bean fields were in full blow, and were likewise overrun with our men, plucking off and chewing the leaves like so many rabbits, devouring them with much greed as a bunch of schoolboys would a plum pudding, after which they filled their haversacks.

---

9   Presumably: it appears the manuscript as Spinhelm.

I took a plentiful supply myself, and found a certain degree of nourishment from them.

At about 2 o'clock I saw a sergeant of the 40th stopping a peasant with a large jug in his hand, who made some resistance. I went to see the cause of the fuss, at which the sergeant decamped. However, I seized the vessel myself, and finding it full of sweetened milk, mixed with fruit, I took my fill without a second thought.

CHAPTER 7

Campo Maior and Elvas

IMMEDIATELY AFTERWARDS, AN ORDER WAS received for us to return to Tomar and follow the 2nd Division to the south, as it was said there was not sufficient strength in the area of Badajoz; but I had assumed that it was more likely due to the lack of provisions, for the 4th Division was leaving Espinhal empty-belly'd.

We set off on 15 March, but covered two leagues only:[1] it was a march I'll never forget, under torrential rain, with men dropping from the ranks all the way, faint from the lack of sustenance; and left where they collapsed with as little concern as if they didn't belong to us. We halted in a plain without trees or shelter and the deluge continued the whole night long. I had got hold of one of the men's packs on which to sit, placing my elbows on my knees and my hands on each side of my head, and in that position I remained until dawn. We were a hungry set of fellows, as no provisions had yet reached us, nor sign of a Commissary; and nothing could be found to eat for love or money.

Next morning we set off for Tomar, reaching within a league of it that evening; but still no Commissary, although several people brought us a little bread from Tomar, together with rice, chocolate, wine, and some spirits. I bought some rice and milk

---

1   This route, then hardly more than a track, would lead almost directly south to Tomar via Cabaços.

which I boiled and afterwards swallowed, mixed with wine and rum, and found it very sustaining; and I saved a good supply for that evening, for the greater part of the division had no means of obtaining anything else except the chocolate, of which they consumed no ordinary quantity, having been starved for three days.

On the 17th we limped into Tomar, where we found our Commissary, and spent the day resting and feasting after our fatigues.[2] Thus restored, we set off next morning to cross the Tagus by a bridge of boats. These had been placed closely wedged against each other from one side of the river to the other and fastened together with ropes, while across them were nailed two broad planks, which provided a secure bridge.

After proceeding four leagues along the south bank, we slept in fields near Arripiado,[3] but as the 4th Division had been ordered to march with all speed to converge with the 2nd, said to be under threat from the garrisons of Campo Maior and Badajoz, we did not let the grass grow under our feet. On the 19th we encamped at Perales;[4] next day at Gavião; and on the following evening near Alpalhão. On the 22nd we reached Portalegre, where we found the 2nd Division together with 4,000 Portuguese cavalry.

We halted here on the 23rd as a greater part of our division was both sore- and bare-footed, and almost un-breached, so that all the tailors and shoemakers among us were placed under

---

2   The 17th was St Patrick's Day, and John Emerson recorded that on that evening many a bumper of aguardiente was tossed off to the raucous singing of 'Ould Ireland' and 'Patrick's day in the morning'.

3   On the south (left) bank of the Tagus opposite Tancos.

4   Its site, on the south bank of the Tagus facing Abrantes, is not apparent on modern maps.

requisition, in order that we would appear both presentable and effective.[5] Meanwhile, the sick or lame were told to fall out and repair to places previously appointed for the reception of the disabled, although very few took advantage of this.

On the 25th we left Portalegre and marched four leagues to Arronches, where we slept, and by 1 o'clock next day we were within two miles of Campo Maior, garrisoned by 7 or 8,000 men. Although surrounded with fortifications, these were not equal in strength to those of either Badajoz or Elvas (the latter in our possession), both being about thirteen miles distant.

*

Bakewell's description of events is here somewhat confused, as he was under the impression that the French, commanded by Marshal Mortier,[6] had re-garrisoned Campo Maior, the Spanish garrison of which had surrendered to the French only a few days earlier after gallantly sustaining a week's bombardment. Mortier did not intend to hold the

---

5   By this time, a proportion of the troops were marching almost barefoot, their shoes or boots being of such poor quality, and it was several weeks before they were re-shod, supplies only reaching them belatedly.

Emerson's description confirms that at Portalegre they 'were served out with a kind of shoes made in the country. They were very clumsy, and if a dirty buff colour; and as many of us were without stockings, their rough seals soon made their wearers hobble like so many cripples.'

There was then no difference between a left or right shoe: a shoe was a shoe. Marc Isambard Brunel (later eminent as a civil engineer), after seeing the lacerated feet of survivors from the Corunna campaign, due to the shoddy footwear previously supplied by unscrupulous manufacturers having rapidly disintegrated, designed a machine to sew stronger boots and shoes and set up a manufactory at Battersea, manned by disabled soldiers. Indeed, when the troops were actually 'on their uppers,' they frequently provided themselves with 'rivilins', moccasins cobbled from hides of cattle they had consumes.

6   Edouard Mortier, Duc de Trévise (1768–1836).

place, but only dismantle it, and transfer any serviceable Portuguese guns to Badajoz. General Latour-Maubourg[7] had been left there with a small force to undertake this task.

William Carr Beresford was now in overall command of all Anglo-Portuguese forces in this southern sector, some 20,000 men altogether.

*

Our general [Beresford], instead of bringing the 2nd and 4th divisions forward, and placing us in a situation where we might have prevented the garrison from escaping from Campo Maior and seeking the security of Badajoz, halted us a mile and a half from the former,[8] and ordered us to wheel to the right to a point at least a mile from the road, where we clustered among some trees. We found the 3rd Dragoon Guards and the 4th Dragoons, commanded by General Long,[9] ahead of us, but dismounted. Here we waited for an hour, kicking our heels, while the garrison sallied out of Campo Maior.

Their infantry might well have been taken prisoners as they veered off about three miles to the right to an unprotected village to await the outcome of their cavalry's expected encounter with ours.[10] By then, theirs had advanced along the Badajoz road, leaving fourteen pieces of artillery

---

7   Marie-Victor-Nicholas de Fay Latour-Maubourg (1768–1850), a distinguished cavalry general, but whose troops were decimated two months' later by Major-General Lumley's Dragoons at Usagre.

8   Oman suggests that Beresford's approach had come as a complete surprise to Mortier, who had made no preparations to meet it, having already withdrawn the majority of his besieging force to Badajoz.

9   Lieutenant Colonel Robert Ballard Long (1771–1821), whose poor employment of cavalry in this action was the subject of controversy and recrimination for several decades.

10   The 'village' may have been no more that a cluster of farm buildings.

behind them,[11] which were captured as the 1st Regiment of Portuguese cavalry and our 13th Light Dragoons engaged with them, making great execution, but not without heavy losses. Then, finding the French were too strong for them, our cavalry were forced to turn back, enabling the enemy to recover their guns.

Meanwhile, the French infantry sallied out from their cover to make good their escape to Badajoz, and had already proceeded about half the distance, when we were instructed to return to the main road and overtake them; but by then it was too late, however rapidly we advanced; indeed impossible, as they were at least seven miles ahead of us. We passed a number of dead and wounded of the cavalry encounter and a pretty sight many of them were, some with split skulls,[12] others with their bowels strewn across the road; for when cavalry is closely engaged – as in this instance – sabres do ghastly execution. However, some of our officers picked up some excellent furniture from the dead French mounts.

We now approached the bridge over the Guadiana, which runs just below Badajoz, only to find that the French had already entered the fortress and closed its gates against us, proof of which was a salvo of artillery from the ramparts.

Our General had let the French secure themselves there without any intervention except by the 1st Portuguese and the 13th British cavalry regiments, losing almost 200 men and prisoners. Had our two infantry divisions been permitted to advance in their support, I have no doubt they would have

---

11 Other sources refer to sixteen guns.

12 This almost certainly refers to Colonel Vital-Joachim Chamorin of the 26th Dragoons, killed in combat with Corporal Logan of the 13th Light Dragoons only twenty days after being promoted to général de brigade, as referred to also in Moyle Sherer's narrative.

taken the whole of the French prisoners and entered Badajoz unmolested,[13] instead of being permitted to remain skulking among those trees, apparently for no other reason but to give the French a chance to escape. A great many in our division were very disappointed, having marched 100 or 150 miles – night and day – to defeat the French, and with apparently every prospect of doing so, only to be thwarted in our expectations due to the whimsical decision of our general to halt us. I wondered how Lord Wellington would make this affair palatable when sending his dispatches to England; but he covered up this wilful negligence better than I expected, for, says he, had it not been for the impetuosity of our 13th Light Dragoons and the 1st Regiment of the Portuguese cavalry, the victory would have been complete; but I believe there would have been no engagement whatever if it had not been for them; and what a slaughter took place before Badajoz afterwards to recover it from the French: some 6 to 7,000 men. Had he but placed our two divisions in the advance of Campo Maior instead of the rear, we should have made the entire garrison prisoners,[14] and gone on to take Badajoz with very little loss.

Beresford's personal appearance is much in his favour, having a darkish aspect; he stands 5ft 11 inches in height, and has very much the resemblance of a warrior apparently just in his prime. He had also acquired a great reputation for training the Portuguese recruits – or at least causing them to be drilled and disciplined – but as a commander of British veterans, he cuts a poor figure; and, as I said then, I thought it would be the

13   John Emerson records that the prisoners taken in this affair 'were intoxicated, having plundered the in habitants of the town [Campo Maior] before its evacuation.'

14   Oman states that the total French force amounted to c. 2,400, half of them being infantry, and including 900 cavalry.

last time he would be chosen for that purpose; and so it has happened.

This is the first day I set foot in Spain, there being a small rivulet — so narrow that I could jump over it — dividing the two kingdoms, which flows about the midway between the two towns, the former being in Portugal, the latter [Badajoz] in Spain.[15]

On returning to Campo Maior, we found the 2nd Division ahead of us, and having all to defile through the gate — there being one entrance only — caused considerable delay, and it was 3.0 before I secured my billet. The town had endured the French occupation with fortitude and, as we entered, the females were frantically waving their handkerchiefs, shouting 'viva English', 'stubborn English', 'no stubborn Francers [sic]', etc.

We remained here from the 26th until the 31st, quitting it next day for Elvas and doubtless to the great relief of the locals, for the old lady upon whom the officers of our company were billeted had been complaining bitterly about how much the French had robbed from her and others. She was the wife of a professional gentleman employed in administering physic. Although they had not taken any of his stock, their house had been cleared of every piece of valuable and portable furniture.[16]

The shells from our artillery, when bombarding the town, had done considerable damage to a great number if the buildings

---

15   I can only think Bakewell is here confusing the Caia with the Guadiana, and assuming that the former marked the frontier.

16   Not only by the French. John Emerson admitted that while in the house in which he was billeted, although they pulled up the floor-boards and torn down ceilings without effect, 'at length some hams were discovered in a draw-well in a corner of a kitchen'; while a few silver spoons, found in the same recess, 'were quickly bartered for wine; and a fire being now made with the furniture, our fatigues were, for a time, forgotten in the noise and luxury of the feast.'

and fortifications,[17] for a shell falling and bursting on the top of a house would effectually demolish the upper storey (as was the case of that I was in); and, if it happened that three or four landed in the same building, there was every likelihood that they would level it to the ground.

While here, I visited several convents and churches and, adjoining one of the latter, I noticed a room singularly furnished, its walls, from floor to ceiling, being entirely inlaid with human bones collected from the nearby burial-grounds: those from legs in the bottom row, on which were piled thighs, arms, skulls, etc., interspersed at intervals of about 4 feet by complete skeletons, which, judiciously placed and admirably polished, caused a curious and unusual effect.[18]

On 31 March I rode my mule to Elvas, where I dined, and returned in the evening; and at 8 o'clock next morning we quit Campo Maior, and at about noon reached Elvas, which must be one of the strongest fortified towns in Europe. It is considered the key to Portugal, and one of the largest cities in the kingdom (with the exception of Lisbon), and has its share of elegant churches, richly adorned internally, and with spacious convents attached to them. The aqueduct here is noted for its great length and height in some places.[19] I followed its course for four and a half miles, expecting to find its source, but it then intermittently disappears. Within a few hundred yards of the town it must be about 160 ft high, and 20 ft wide; though the height varies

---

17   Again, Bakewell is mistaken: the damage was caused when the French besieged the fortress.

18   Several of these gruesome ossuaries or charnel-houses survive in Portugal, the entrances to which are not infrequently inscribed 'Nos ossos que aqui estamos, pelos vossos esperamos (these bones are waiting for yours!)'

19   The imposing 'Aqueduto da Amoreira', with its huge cylindrical buttresses, dates largely from the sixteenth century.

with the inequalities of the ground. From the spring, the water flows along a channel some 4 to 5 ft in circumference into a huge cistern, which is supposed to contain enough water to keep the inhabitants supplied for six months, should the fortress be besieged. The aqueduct would no doubt be the first object of the enemy, and cutting off the water supply would be very easy. I wonder why they never ran pipes underground, as the expense would be a good deal less, and the security much greater. They were sinking a well in the hope of finding a spring, but as the town is situated on a hill I don't suppose they will ever accomplish it, for they had already reached a depth of several hundred feet.

Outside the walls, to the south-east, rises Fort St Lucia; but the more considerable one is what they call Fort Le Lippe.[20] Although Elvas itself is built on a height encircled by walls, this fort is even higher. Its defences are immensely strong, with cannon being placed at appropriate distances along what may be compared to a winding stair-case, from which positions – being one above the other – they can discharge three or four projectiles at a time; and the sheer height of this fort is so great that one is obliged to wind round it two or three times before reaching the summit. When he gets there, he will find accommodation for 10,000 men, making it almost impossible to take if defended by that number. Should it be taken, it would be either for lack of water, provisions or ammunition. From the summit, and also from the convents within Elvas, with a telescope one may discern the French very plainly both in Badajoz and at the fort of St Christopher (San Cristóbal), about

---

20   Fort Santa Lucia dates from the seventeenth century; and the other, originally 'da Graça', dominating the town from the north, was completed in the late 18th century after the design of Count William Schaumberg-Lippe (1724–77), an English-born German, who had previously reorganised the Portuguese army.

quarter of a mile this side of it, both being east of us. Fort Le Lippe, commanding a view of several leagues in all directions, is so naturally strong and artfully improved, as to be virtually inaccessible, although it would be possible to starve the garrison of Elvas by preventing the entry of all supplies.

CHAPTER 8

Olivenza

WE LEFT ELVAS ON 4 April and proceeded south to within a league of Juromenha, a large village overlooking the river Guadiana, and fortified, as it appears were all the frontier town of these two kingdoms, though it is not as strong as some others. We here encamped, and next day I took my mule and rode into town, which we marched through at 8.0 on the 6th on our descent to the Guadiana, where we found four large open boats waiting to ferry us over.

The river here is nearly the width as is the Thames at the Tower,[1] but its current is much stronger. The 27th was the first regiment to cross, and we waited on the opposite bank until the 97th had joined us, when we were ordered to advance a league further to the village of Villarreal, expecting the others to follow soon after.[2] On halting within a few hundred yards of it, we were instructed to sleep on our arms; the officers to remain within ten paces of the line, and none of us – commissioned or not – were to take off our accoutrements. Vedettes and pickets

---

1   It was c. 180 yards wide here. For a succinct description of the crossing and ensuing operations at Olivenza, in which the author refers to several accounts, see Peter Edwards's *Albuera*.

2   D'Urban refers to the army having bivouacked 'by Brigades in succession as it had crossed, in a position of Assembly, of which the Right was upon and beyond Villa Real, on a boggy rivulet, and the Left upon the Guadiana and which formed an angle at about 1½ English Miles on the road from Villa Real to Badajoz and thus fronted both Badajoz and Olivenza . . .'

were sent forward, and as the regimental guards were in place by 1 o'clock, Sampson, and Lieutenant Thomas Coppinger[3] of the 97th proposed that, to shelter from the wind, we should sneak into one of village houses – which we did, although contrary to orders. We found it empty except for a few chairs and tables, on one of which I slept, while Coppinger dossed down on the ground below me. We were followed shortly by half a dozen other officers, who lay around the room; but we didn't rest for long, for at about 3.0, Coppinger, pulling at my coat, awoke me to say that the enemy was in the street, where firing as thick as hail was soon heard. Grabbing our hats (cocked ones were then our regimental ones), we sallied forth to regain the regiment where we had left it, some quarter of a mile distant, by then forming up under General Cole himself, who as we came up thundered out: 'For God Almighty's sake men, form yourselves or else it will be all over with us.' This we did immediately and, once ready to move, he ordered the two flank companies of both regiments to follow him towards the sound of firing and discover where the enemy lay. These 400 advanced up the nearest street,[4] the remaining sixteen companies having been ordered to circle round and to meet us at the far end of the village. Before we met up with them, our flank companies made one charge, to find that the French had fled already, nor did we expect to see them again that night.

But suddenly, balls were flying around us in all directions, and Captain William Dobbin, commanding the company, says: 'Bakewell, we must now either bite the dust or be dragged to a French prison: damn a pin if I was given to choose.' As we had no knowledge of their strength, we naturally concluded

---

3   Lieutenant Coppinger was wounded at the sortie from Badajoz on 10 May.

4   It has little more than one street!

Map 2: A French plan of Olivenza (detail)

that they had watched us crossing the Guadiana, and as we were only two regiments, had surrounded us. However, a volley from our men dispersed them. Cole now halted us, and here we stood prepared to act on the defensive until daylight. That enemy bullets were the first warning of their approach was rather an unprecedented case, and we could not understand what could have had prevented out pickets and outlying vedettes from giving us warning that the enemy was so close. I must confess that it was a relief to hear the French bugles sound a retreat.

Daylight gave us a better idea of the weakness of our position and how lucky we were to have escaped. As other stragglers came in, giving their accounts of the surprise, we were told that three French regiments – two of cavalry and one infantry, part of Olivenza's garrison – out foraging, had left their place of rendezvous, hoping to amass more plunder.[5] By chance, they had bumped into a Portuguese unit rather too far in advance, which they surrounded and took prisoner. Moving forward cautiously, they had stumbled on a vedette of fifty men of our 13th Light Dragoons, dismounted and feeding their horses at the time, whom likewise they compelled to surrender.[6] They

------

5   Bakewell had noted that the town, as Olivença, together with a few adjacent villages on the left bank of the Guadiana here, originally a Portuguese enclave, had been ceded by treaty to Spain. This had occurred in 1801, after the so-called 'War of the Oranges', when the Spanish occupied it; but despite provision in the 1814 Treaty of Paris that they should return it to Portugal, this was never implemented. Its former

Governor, General Manuel Herck, a Swiss, had surrendered to Soult only three months previously, on the 23rd January after a brief siege, and it had been re-garrisoned under Colonel Jean Niboyet or Neboyer.

6   This would have been Major Redmond Morres's squadron. It is of interest that Captain William Bragge (3rd Dragoons), writing home from Belém in early September, refers to having 'heard of another Party of the Eleventh

then proceeded to attack a picket commanded by Lieutenant Mangin, and had seized his horse, but not him: seeing that he was outnumbered, he had hidden, but several of his men were wounded. This force then attacked our line, but did little injury; and, from the haste with which they quit the field, it would seem that they were as ignorant of our strength as we were of theirs.

It was about 8.0 next morning that the 40th Regiment joined us, and we learned that the French had made good their retreat into Olivenza after taking some 150 of our men prisoner, due to being surprised and the fact that many of them – contrary to orders, which were to sleep on their arms – having pulled off their packs and made pillows of them, had left them on the ground in their haste to grab their muskets; and when they regained their former position, found to their mortification that the local peasantry had made off with them. It was fortunate that General Cole was with us, as in this instance Brigadier General Kemmis,[7] who had he been present, would have been accountable for this affair, but I believe he was with the 40th Regiment in our rear, as he belonged to it. He might have brought us through, but Cole was our favourite.

---

consisting of a Sergt, 2 Corporals and twelve Privates being surprised and taken by the French, making [it] the Third Picquet they have lost; and as no Man or Officer of this Regt has ever been on Duty near the Enemy's Post, I fear some of us will share the same Fate ere long.'

7   Major General James Kemmis (Montmellick, Leix. 1751–1821 Cheltenham), older than the majority of Wellington's generals, had first served as an Ensign in the 9th Foot in 1775. He had taken part in several foreign expeditions and, more recently, he had seen action at Talavera. At Busaco, his brigade (3/27th, 40th, 97th and one company of the 5/60th), forming part of Cole's 4th Division, defended the left flank of the Allied line, but suffered no casualties. Kemmis had been widowed in 1810

We halted at Villarreal on the 7th and 8th and, next day – all our strength having now made good their passage of the Guadiana – we advanced to attack Olivenza. The 4th Division was preceded by the 2nd, and at about noon, when within a mile of it, we formed a two-deep line in the shape of a half circle to its west, north-west, and south-west. It being strongly fortified, with a garrison of nearly 1,000 men, was the reason we kept at a distance while fatigue parties were sent ahead to raise earthworks, which they did despite continuous gun-fire; but as it was getting dark by then it did very little damage although they were not more than a musket shot from the ramparts. The only hazard to the fatigue parties was the chance of being hit while relieving each other, which was every twelve hours; but meanwhile these works, thrown up to protect our artillery, were proceeding well, although our guns had not yet arrived.

Olivenza, with some 5,000 inhabitants, is similar to the other frontier towns,[8] but the fortifications are by no means as strong as those of either Elvas or Badajoz. Its walls, 7 or 8 yards thick, are quite high, while spaced out evenly on the terreplein opposite their embrasures, stood their cannon. The walls, the circuit of which is continuous, are pierced at each entrance by three pairs of gates – or more properly, six – one on either side of the ramparts. If and when besieged, they could close the outer gate, which opened inwards, and fill the intervening space with earth, making them almost as strong as any other part of the circumvallation.

On the 10th, a detachment from the 2nd Division was placed in a position to stop any supplies which might attempt to reach

---

8   An interesting account of Olivença as it was in October–December 1809 has been left in the Letters of Sir George Ridout Bingham when stationed there after the retreat from Talavera.

the garrison; which they did, intercepting a convoy some seven miles away, and seizing 30,000 rations, which would have come in very useful to the garrison.

Next morning, the 11th, General Beresford summoned the Governor of Olivenza to surrender, but he refused; and as our artillery had still not arrived – nor did we know when it might – there was little we could do. Beresford then advanced the 2nd Division, leaving Cole with the 4th to take Olivenza. On the 12th, I planned to make the circuit of the fortifications, it being open country, though taking care to ride well out of range of their cannonades, least one might tumble me, but I found the distance much longer than I had expected, and was not sorry to get back.

The 27th, together with the 11th Portuguese, were on guard next morning (two regiments being on duty the whole time the siege lasted, relieved every twenty-four hours), being relieved by the 7th Fusiliers and the 23rd Portuguese, which had been stationed on a hill just out of cannon-range,[9] which gave them a view over Olivenza; and it would have been impossible for the garrison to have made their escape without us noticing their preparations to do so.

On the morning of the 14th (Easter Sunday) we were relieved by the 23rd and our 40th. Our artillery arrived next day and started firing the moment they were mounted behind the prepared fieldworks.[10] By 2.0, the French had sent out a

---

9   Probably the Atalaya de Donna Anna.

10   The artillery was commanded by Major Alexander Dickson, who together with Captain John Squire of the Engineers (arriving on the 10th) reconnoitred the place, agreeing on which appeared to be the weakest section of the walls to batter. Oman IV, p. 272, states that the six 24-pounders had been brought from Elvas, but as the cask-bridge at Juromenha was not strong enough to bear them, they had to be ferried over on flying-bridges,

flag of truce and asked to treat; but our General would accept unconditional submission only, giving them half an hour to decide whether or not to submit. As no reply had been received by then, he ordered our artillery to recommence; and they soon made a practical breach,[11] doing substantial damage. At the time (about 3.0), I happened to be standing quite close to General Cole, when he gave a sudden start, exclaiming 'By God, they have surrendered,' called for his horse and, followed by his staff, rode immediately into the town. I could not understand how he already knew this, until I saw a white flag hoisted on a steeple.[12]

Later on, I entered the place to procure some provisions and, on my return to the regiment, found myself being followed by 400 prisoners that had just surrendered and were drawn up about ten yards in front of us. They were ordered to drop their packs and, leaving them open, turn to the right about and halt ten yards away. Our men then paced forward and having been told to take what they wanted from the bulging packs, found a deal of plunder, notably sheets, table cloths, and other linen, apart from valuables and curiosities.[13] We helped ourselves to most of the contents, found very seasonable: for the linen

---

but had only opened fire the next morning (15th), when 70 rounds each was enough to make a practicable breach . According to D'Urban, Mr Ogilvie of the Commissariat was also sent to Elvas to hasten the belated arrival of food supplies, which were running short.

11   The term 'practicable' meant that infantry could enter it with comparative ease. D'Urban refers to each of the five 24-pounders having fired 72 rounds.

12   In reporting to Beresford, Cole refers to this being hoisted at 11 o'clock. D'Urban gives the same time.

13   John Emerson had commented that their knapsacks 'were destitute of anything of value, the Frenchman secreting money, trinkets, or the like, in a kind of belt worn next to the skin.'

served to make plenty of pantaloons and gaiters; and the knives, spoons, etc. were of good quality. Once we had reaped our harvest, the French were told to face front and pick up their bundles (relieved of much of their burden), and that evening, escorted by Portuguese units, they were marched away on their long journey to England.

We acquired 15 pieces of artillery, principally of small calibre; the muskets of 800 men; and rounded up 400 additional prisoners, many of whom were ill.[14] The 97th garrisoned the place that evening, relieved next day by a Portuguese regiment. If our artillery had come up at the same time as our cavalry and infantry, we would have taken the place sooner; however, our loss was trifling, with very few killed and only thirty to forty wounded.

Once the 4th Division had secured their trophies,[15] they followed the 2nd, as it was said that we were to proceed to Seville to meet Sir Thomas Graham after he had fought the battle of Barrosa,[16] at which he had 4,000 men, exclusive of 3,000 Spaniards who had joined him after landing at Cadiz. Confronted by a French force of 8,000, he had attacked them, expecting that the Spaniards would support his troops; but instead of participating in the engagement, they had halted upon a hill some distance away, eye-witnesses of his victory

---

14   Oman IV, p. 271 states that there were 96, attended by 16 surgeons.

15   This was two days after a consignment of shoes reached them – none having been found at Elvas – badly needed before they could move, many of the troops being entirely unshod after their recent long marches.

Wellington, on hearing of the surrender of Olivenza, had written to congratulate Beresford, adding; 'I entirely concur in the directions which you gave that the garrison should have no terms; and I hope they were well plundered by the 4th division . . .'

16   General Sir Thomas Graham (1748–1843), one of the very few of his generals in whom Wellington had entire confidence.

against so unequal a force without having cooperated an iota, although they afterwards joined him.[17]

We quit the field of Olivenza on the morning of the 16th, and marched five leagues to Almendral, where we bivouacked, and after another four and a half leagues next day, halted just short of Santa Marta, which I entered to lay in a fresh stock of provisions. Apparently, the 13th Light Dragoons had taken two French cavalry officers prisoner, who were most elegantly dressed, as I saw them myself through the gates of their place of detention; and they had also liberated twenty of our Dragoons which had been captured at Villarreal. They had been in the company of 100 French cavalry, which were now safely lodged under an escort from the 2nd Division.

We remained at Santa Marta on the 19th, and were told next morning to return along the road by which we had come, an order which we assumed had came from Headquarters, due to his Lordship's determination not to leave Badajoz in our rear and in the possession of the enemy, but to drive the French out and clear the country before him. The right brigade of the 4th Division was the first to leave Santa Marta, and we bivouacked at Almendral again that evening, next day marching to Valverde [de Leganés], where we formed our lines, and here we remained on the 22nd.

It was surprising to see the difference between the people of the two kingdoms, despite their proximity, for the Portuguese are somewhat in the Dutch mould, being rather under-sized,

---

17   Obviously, this description was added later by Bakewell on receiving hearsay reports of the action at Barrosa (often incorrectly spelt as Barossa), which had taken place south of Cadiz on 5 March. The pusillanimity of the Spanish general, Manuel La Peña, who had kept his troops immobile within earshot of the battle, and then later had the audacity to claim the victory, was more than Graham could stomach.

stiff built, and bottom-heavy, while the Spanish appears to be more athletic, tall and well-proportioned, but I realise that I am referring to their general physical characteristics, and not as individuals, for there are exceptions in both cases.

The Spanish ladies have generally good and genteel figures, but they are not as fair as the British ones: the climate being so much hotter, the sun darkens their complexions. As side-saddles are not used here at all, when they ride, they ride astride as do the men, and wear drawers of a kind of calico. They dress expensively, and are great people for wearing feathers.

CHAPTER 9

From Juromenha to Badajoz

ON THE MORNING OF 23 April we quit Valverde; skirted Olivenza; and at about 4.0 reached the Guadiana, where we found a temporary bridge erected for our conveyance as before.[1] It was a curious structure, fabricated as follows: two empty casks, each about the size of half hogsheads, were fastened together with ropes, and floated close to the bank. Another two were tied together at about 8 or 9 ft from the first, and so on at similar intervals from one side of the river to the other, and all held together by means of ropes stretched right across. On these floating casks were nailed two planks (their lengths depending to the size of the casks); and, on one side of the fabrication, a kind of [rope?] railing had been fixed for us to slide our hands along, as the current was very strong.

Our Grenadier Company commenced their march over this dancing bridge, but when they reached the third section, the ropes gave way, and the men on it would have lost their balance and been precipitated into the river had they not clung to the railing, and the only loss was that of a few muskets. On regaining dry land, they had to wait for fifteen minutes or so while the ropes were re-adjusted, before recommencing their precarious passage along this bridge, which happened to carry all of us over safely, as it did the 97th Regiment, which followed. Unfortunately, just as they had cleared it and the 40th was

---

1   This had been rigged up by Captain John Squire, R.E.

about to start over, a sudden boisterous swell arose, sweeping away the whole: casks, ropes, and railing went floating away down-stream, to the consternation of those who happened to be watching the scene.

We were now in an unpleasant situation, for the baggage and provisions of both the 27th and 97th remained on the far bank to the rear of the 40th. We had not so much as a change of linen with us, nor was there any chance of it reaching us for some time as Badajoz, in enemy hands, was the nearest river crossing. The next bridge was some 40 miles further up-stream at Merida, to which we were now ordered to make our way as best we could. Both the 97th, on one bank, and the 40th, together with the provisions and clothing for the whole brigade, on the other, had no alternative to making a circuitous march to avoid Badajoz, in case the garrison make a sortie and attacked either: they would be too strong for us, divided as we were. The 40th returned to Villa Real to sleep, while the rest of us were billeted on the villagers of Juromenha without food, for nothing could be got here except chocolate, although of that there was plenty.

Next morning, as the 40th were skirting the left bank,[2] we made our way above the right, entering Elvas at about noon, where we billeted, and next day reached Campo Maior, where we remained – I in my old billet – on the 26th and 27th. On the following day we marched east towards the extensive woods of Alburquerque, to bivouac near a river [the Zapatón] well stocked with fish, and we caught a quantity from ½ to 2 lb in weight, which came in handy. Frustrated by being without their baggage, the officers spent most of the night carousing and drinking grog, those without any being supplied by those who had; but what most inconvenienced us was the lack of utensils.

---

2   They would have to give Badajoz itself a wide berth likewise before bearing east parallel to the Guadiana to approach Merida.

After having cooked our fish, we set fire to the roots of a tree and sat around enjoying ourselves until daylight, when we left the tree which had given us heat and light all night to smoulder, and continued our route to Montijo,[3] where we halted for two days.

Meanwhile, on 2 May, having crossed the bridge at Merida that day,[4] the 40th joined us, bringing our baggage, and not before time, for we had had no change of clothes for ten days.

Orders reached us next morning that one officer from each regiment should report to Elvas, where a Depot would be established and where they would be stationed under a field officer, as the French had become increasingly restless. In the event, this duty fell on me, and I set off from Montijo at 5 o'clock on the 4th. It was a long march, taking me close to Badajoz, but out of range of their guns. Meanwhile, a Portuguese tradesman with a couple of mules — riding one while leading the other — on seeing my horse carrying my luggage being led by my servant, offered me one of his mules to ride, which I accepted. But in the next valley, which was water-logged to a depth of several feet, the mule chose to lie down, leaving me to dismount in the water up to the middle! I left him there to be fetched by his master, and continued on foot to Campo Maior, reached by about 6.0 that evening, and repaired to my old billet.

I reported for duty at Elvas early next morning, and the Commandant there, Captain Brown,[5] introduced me to

---

3   Montijo is a small town on a branch of the Guadiana, about half-way between Merida and Badajoz.
4   This would have been the 64-arch long Roman bridge. Two arches were broken down in the following year to retard Marmont's attempted relief of Badajoz, but no move was made by the Spanish to repair them until 1835.
5   Captain Peter Brown (23rd).

Lieutenants Hawkins and Griffiths,[6] two officers from his regiment, the 23rd Fusiliers, with whom I dined. I found that my duties were to visit each officer and man of the 27th once a day to enquire if the doctor's attendance was also daily, if they had any complaints, and to ensure that they received their rations regularly; to forward those men to the regiment once the doctors had certified them as being well enough; to attend parades at 11.0 each day, and to report weekly to the regiment on those who were sick. These, while I was there, were one captain, two subalterns, one surgeon, one sergeant, eight corporals, and seventy-five privates, making a total of eighty-eight.

I found myself very comfortably installed, having a couple of rooms at an excellent billet, where I could entertain my friends agreeably; and when I needed provisions and wine, I had only to send my servant to the store where he bought what I wanted; and as one of our corporals issued the drink, he used to supply it from the best cask.[7]

On 8 May, the 2nd and 4th divisions on the south-east side of Badajoz commenced their attack, the right brigade of the 4th, consisting of not less than 3,000 men of the 27th, the 97th and the 40th, being placed on the north-west side. As the Guadiana flowed just outside the town gate, should they be attacked, this brigade would be unable to join the rest of the besieging force, as there was no way of crossing the river except by the bridge,

---

6   Lieutenants Thomas Hawkins and William Griffiths

7   Note that James McGrigor (1771–1858) did not reach the Peninsula, as Inspector General of Hospitals, until the following January, after which the state of hospital depots, and medical attention in general begin to improve very considerable, and Bakewell would not have had such a comfortable time. The reader is referred to the narratives of Cooper, Costello, and William Green among others.

which was in French possession and protected by the ramparts; but they could fall back to the security of Elvas.

As soon as it was dark on the first evening, fatigue parties were sent forward to a proper distance and began raising fieldworks for our artillery, and made considerable progress; but there was what they named Fort San Cristóbal, on the same side of the river as our brigade, which annoyed them greatly. Strongly defended, this stood on a hill which, due to its elevation, commanded that north side of Badajoz.

That evening, Major General Kemmis of the 40th, commanding the brigade, sent forward a relief to the fatigue party. It had almost completed its task, when the garrison made a sortie, intent on forcing them away and levelling the earthworks already erected. Captain John Smith, in command of the covering troops, immediately went to their aid and succeeded in driving back the enemy, but at some loss, sacrificing his own life when a heavy shot took off his head just as he had regained possession of the ground they had lost. Major John Birmingham of the 27th, now given command of the six flank companies of the three regiments, was able to thrust the French back within the walls, but the flower of his brigade, while retiring to their own lines, were mowed down by fire from the fortifications. Among them was the major, hit by a shell which took away the lower part of his belly. Together with 113 rank and file wounded, he was taken back on spring wagons to Elvas and placed in my care, but died at 3.0 that morning. The killed lay where they fell, except those that may have rolled into the adjacent ditch.

On the 9th, the fatigue party recommenced their exertions, which continued next day. Meanwhile, we were not idle at the Depot, for the numbers of wounded arriving had increased our work very considerably. Amongst our duties was to get coffins made for the officers, for the inhabitants had never made one, and it was only with difficulty we could make them understand their shape and construction. The first they ran up was for a Lieutenant Castile.[8] We placed him within, nailed down the lid, and a fatigue party from the 23rd started to carry him downstairs but, on the descent, his feet pushed out one end and his body slipped through and fell to the bottom, leaving the empty coffin on their shoulders! We had one of superior stamp made for our departed major. At burials, the officers would alternately take over the duty of officiating as clergymen, although this was carried out in rather an abridged form.

On the morning of 11 May a detachment of convalescents was ordered to descend to our lines before Badajoz. As Lieutenant Bowen of the 40th,[9] whose turn it was to take command, could not be found, this devolved on me. I set off at about 8 o'clock with some forty men of three regiments. We had gone about three miles when I met four men carrying a blanket, the corners of which were fastened to long staves, held quite high. I asked who they had there, to be told: 'Your Colonel, Sir'. I rode up, saying that I hoped he was not much hurt, at which Colonel Maclean himself replied that he was only shot in the thigh, but hoped he would soon be able to resume the command, and asked me to call on him the moment I was back in Elvas. I continued the journey and, two miles beyond, overtook some wagons conveying wine to the besiegers. As three or four of the casks appeared to be leaking badly, I ordered my detachment to fill their canteens with however much they wanted; but they did not drink to excess or get intoxicated, otherwise we would have never reached our destination.

---

8   Unidentified. Bakewell had commented that the coffin had been made in the shape of a long box, its sides being parallel to each other!
9   Lieutenant Edward Cole Bowen, later Captain.

I found the 27th at about noon, with Major Erskine[10] in command, due to our colonel being wounded. Having seen that those in the detachment had joined their respective regiments, I stayed and dined with him before returning to Elvas. Next morning, I found a great addition to my lot of wounded, among the officers being Captain Pring,[11] shot in the groin, and they could not extract the ball; Lieutenant Hanby,[12] shot through the thigh; and Ensign McCoard, shot in the hip. The latter was attacked by spasms and, likewise, the ball could not be extracted, and he afterwards died.[13] The losses in the 40th and 97th were as severe as in our own.

Skirmishing continued with varied success until, on 14 May, orders were given to raise the siege, as General Soult was hastening to relieve the garrison with a force of 20,000 men.

---

10   Major William Howe Knight Erskine (1782–1843). He retired on half-pay in 1813.

11   Captain John Pring.

12   Lieutenant Featherstone Hanby: he was also to be wounded at Sorauren.

13   As Bakewell noted: 'In addition to those officers I have already mentioned of the 27th that were wounded, the following were slightly: Lieutenants Charles Levinge, and Francis Simcoe (both of whom were killed at the storming of Badajoz, 6 April 1812), William Dobbin, Philip Gordon, and Mangin.'

CHAPTER 10

La Albuera

THE RIGHT BRIGADE OF THE 4th Division left their cannon at Elvas, and immediately set off to join the rest of the division, while the left joined the 2nd Division. As there was no convenient passage over the Guadiana except at Juromenha, they had almost a thirty-mile march before they could reach the lines on the south side of Badajoz. Elvas was traversed at 2 o'clock on the morning of the 15th, but as General Beresford did not think it politic to wait for this reinforcement, they were ordered to advance at once to engage the enemy on the field of Albuera[1] next day, where at about 10 o'clock a most bloody battle commenced between the two contending armies.

I suppose Albuera is about sixteen or seventeen miles as the crow flies from Elvas, and as the site may be seen across flattish country, I climbed to the summit of one of the convents with a group of friars and priests who had had chairs placed there. Here I sat from 11.0 until 4.0, and could plainly see the battlefield with my naked eye; but as we had several telescopes with us and being a fine day,[2] the progress of the battle could be clearly observed; but the smoke that arose from their musketry was the truest guide. When I left my post of observation, the combatants were in the same state as I first found them.

---

1   Correctly, La Albuera.

2   Curious: most narratives refer to a sudden rain-storm, but they may have been very local.

My duties at this time were very heavy, having over 300 disabled rank and file of 27th dispersed in various billets and convents throughout Elvas. As the numbers were increasing daily, I found it almost impossible to make out a report of their numbers with any accuracy, for instead of applying to the Officer Commanding when they first arrived (which was what they should have done), they would take the first billet they could find; and, as long as they could obtain medical attendance and provisions they made no claim on me nor gave any notice of their presence.

But to return to the battle, fought until the evening, when both armies retired to the ground from which they had advanced. I am told that had it not been for the three fusilier battalions – that is two of the 7th and one of the 23rd – in all probability the French would have triumphed. Our infantry were attacked for the first time by what they called the Polish Lancers, which succeeded in breaking their lines – one of the very few instances that this happened – and a great part of the 3rd Regiment (commonly named 'The Buffs') were made prisoner. Their lances were long in the handle, similar to a sergeant's halberd, the end fixed in a case forming part of a belt buckled round the body; and the regiment, thus armed, were also intoxicated to boost their courage; while our infantry, not expecting this unusual attack, unexpectedly gave way when on the point of grounding their arms. As soon as they had recovered from the panic which this unprecedented charge had caused, they turned to the right about and gave them a very serious lesson; but by the end of the action there were very few left to boast of their achievements.

The three fusilier battalions, forming part of our Light Division, annihilated the three French regiments opposed to them, and on approaching three others from reserves sent in to replace their losses, the Fusilier brigade gave them such a volley that caused them to turn right about, and in their pursuit up a long ascent, they were very nearly destroyed by the time the hill was recovered. (In the evening, as if moved by the same instinct, both armies retired to the same ground that they had held previously – so it might be said that neither side could boast of much – and remained drawn up in order of battle as before.)

At about 5 o'clock the right brigade of the 4th Division, consisting of the 27th, 40th, and 97th regiments, reached our lines,[3] and it was said that each man in that line was ordered to deploy 5 yards from the next, so that when it opened up to admit the men of our three regiments, it became much extended; and that the moment the French saw this additional force preparing to advance, they commenced their retreat, leaving many of their wounded behind them, several pieces of artillery, and most of the prisoners they had taken – principally from the Buffs. These, both officers and men, had been stripped of their accoutrements and headgear, and returned to us bare-headed. The few remaining in French hands were sent back in a similar state two or three days later, but they had no complaint of the treatment they received.

The enemy having fled, gave our men the chance of surveying the field on which the slaughter had taken place: the dead lay in heaps: some 2,290 from our lines alone, and 4,200 wounded were sent back to Elvas.[4] Lieutenant Philip Gordon said that he was never more surprised than to see the men on either side lying dead in their ranks, as regularly placed as if they had been living, and thus one might plainly see where each regiment had been stationed. A trench was made, 500 or 600 yards long and

---

3   These included part of Kemmis's brigade: Light companies of the 2/27th, 1/40th, and 1/97th only.

4   Bakewell's figures are exaggerated, when compared to recent calculations, as in Guy Dempsey's *Albuera 1811*, particularly as to those killed.

4 or 5 yards wide, where they buried many, and the remainder were placed in a heap and burned, together with plenty of wood, lest the atmosphere be contaminated by the stench from these corpses.[5]

Those which sustained most loses were the second battalions of the 7th and 48th regiments, and first battalions of the 23rd, 28th, 29th, 31st, 34th, 57th, and 66th. The 3rd had at one time suffered heavily in numbers until those taken prisoner regained their liberty, by which it recovered much of its strength. Each of the 66th, 3rd, and 48th regiments lost one of their colours, trophies which the French made no little boast of securing.

I saw Captain Chesslyn of the 13th Portuguese belonging to our 48th[6] – who is a brother to squire Langly, about two miles from here[7] – who said that they were some shy cocks upon that occasion; amongst others he mentioned were a Major [Henry] King, and a Colonel Stewart of the 3rd,[8] who was leaving Elvas on the evening and about the time the engagement was drawing to its close; but there was a subaltern named Hare, belonging to the 27th, who surpassed most of my acquaintances.

He had previously marched with me through Ireland, but refused to embark. I found him secreted in a billet at Elvas, where he had been for some time, drawing his pay from the *Juiz de Fora*,[9] in consequence, as he said, of being on

---

5   As described by Alexander Gordon, writing from Elvas on 24 May: 'We were over the ground the other day, the slaughter was immense, there were over 3,000 naked bodies lying on the field.'

6   This was Lieutenant William W. Chesslyn (or Cheslyn), from May 1812 a captain in the 48th, who had served previously as a captain in the Portuguese 13th Line, and had been severely wounded at Talavera.

7   Castle Donington, Bakewell's home town, confirming that he would have written up his notes there.

8   Lieutenant Colonel William Stewart (1769–1854)

9   Justice of the Peace.

the sick list; but his regiment had not the least knowledge of him being in the country, although he had been here for some months. When I mentioned this to Sir John Maclean, he ordered me to tell Hare that he was appointed to take command of the first detachment of the regiment that left Elvas, which occurred within a few days. Thus he set out with them after previously calling on the wounded colonel, who was still here; but, three or four days afterwards, I found him back in his old billet. When asked why he had returned, he replied that on the road he had met some young men that had been wounded at Albuera, several without arms, some without legs, and some of them possibly might have no heads: having seen more than enough, had passed on the command to the sergeant. This was also enough for our Colonel, on the advice of a board, to send him back to England, where he was dispossessed of his commission. But there must always be such characters as he was.

When all these wounded reached Elvas, the whole town appeared to have been converted into one big hospital.[10] General Hoghton had been killed, and was brought here for interment.[11] He had received one shot through his left shoulder; but the second was in his right breast, which proved mortal. The officers here were all ordered to attend his funeral, where we saw him before the lid on the coffin was fastened; and he was honoured with the cannon firing the customary salute from the ramparts. Colonel Duckworth was likewise killed,[12] and Major

---

10   A number of the wounded had been taken also to both Valverde (where Surgeon Guthrie was stationed) and Olivenza.

11   Major General Daniel Hoghton (1770–1811) is buried in the military cemetery at Elvas.

12   Lieutenant Colonel George Henry Duckworth (1782–1811), 48th Foot; a son of Admiral Sir John Duckworth.

Brooke of the 48th was assumed to be,[13] as he was missing and never seen afterwards; and there were many other field and commissioned officers. Major General Cole had a shot in the breach, and his whole staff were wounded; General Stewart,[14] *et al*; the whole loss on this occasion was said to be 7,000 including those killed and wounded. The French did not escape without suffering losses equally severe, having had two generals killed, two others wounded, and many commissioned officers of lower rank, as their total casualties were supposed to have been 10,000, including the disabled with the killed.[15]

The French retreated along the road to Seville, closely pursued by our cavalry, which succeeded in cutting off small parties and forwarding them as prisoners to the Depots. The strength of the British lines when *first* engaged did not exceed 20,000, exclusive of 7,000 Spanish cavalry,[16] while it was said that the enemy numbers were 35,000.[17]

It would seem that our General Beresford did not obtain many additional laurels on this occasion, for he over-calculated his own strength, and at the same time underrated that of the enemy; and it was said that had it not been for our Light Division

---

13   Major William Brooke. In fact, he was taken prisoner, but managed to escape from Seville and rejoined his regiment in mid August, only to be severely wounded at the storming of Badajoz on 6 April 1812, when serving on the Staff as AQMG. See under Oman in the Bibliography.

14   Major General the Hon. William Stewart (1774–1827) was only slightly wounded, and more severely in the Pyrenees on 25 July 1813.

15   According to Oman, and confirmed by Dempsey, total Allied casualties were just over 5,900; those of the French being a very few more, but the percentage of losses among them was much higher. Bakewell's figure, as far as the Allies are concerned, may include many whose wounds would be mortal.

16   More like 3,700.

17   Soult's army numbered c. 22,850 men in all.

and the Spanish cavalry,[18] which on this occasion did much execution, the result of the engagement might have been very different. Their undaunted courage and persevering bravery contributed to a great degree to our success. It is not often that we can commend the conduct of the Spaniards in the field, but in this instance they fought nobly; and the victory was obtained by no other means except hard blows and fierce obstinacy.

The 2nd and the 4th divisions remained in the field for some days after, as there was a deal of reorganization necessary and a variety of duties to perform after such a battle in preparation for the next engagement, for it was thought very likely that the French might return.

During this period Lord Wellington, together with his staff, rode south to Elvas from the neighbourhood of Almeida, leaving instructions for his units there to follow at speed, with the exception of one division;[19] and they reached us quite soon after, having marched in quick time. On arrival, Lord Wellington immediately took command, determined to attack Badajoz again.

This second attempt was to be made by the 3rd and 7th divisions, with the 2nd and 4th being placed between them and the French under Soult. During these preparations we were very busy at the Depot, for such a crowded scene of confusion amongst such a multitude if disabled military is not often to be met with.

I went one morning to see the medical gentlemen attempt to extract the ball from McCoard.[20] It had entered the inside

18   Bakewell is probably here referring to Alten's independent brigades of the KGL.

19   Commanded by General Sir Brent Spencer.

20   Ensign James McCoard of the 27th is listed as being wounded during the repulse of a sortie at Badajoz on 10 May: he died on the 27th.

of his thigh just above the knee, but they could not find where it had lodged, and had probed several inches but still could not reach it. The surgeon then proposed amputating his leg, and then decided not to; but when he died a few days later, and the wound was opened, it was found that the ball had penetrated to the hip, where that part of it which had hit the bone was quite flat, which satisfied them that amputation would have had no effect, as the ball would have remained thus embedded. I got a coffin made and had him buried the morning after his death; and prevailed on two or three officers of the 23rd to accompany me to the place of interment. Never did I smell anybody so offensive, for we could not march within twenty paces of the corpse, due I supposed to its mortification in this hot country. One of the officers read over the service while we put him to bed and there left him. There was about one acre of ground, walled around, about half a mile outside the walls of Elvas which was allotted as the place of burial for British officers.[21]

Next day, I took an inventory of his effects: a gold watch; a little jewellery; and a bond for £200, which I sent to the Major commanding: the clothing, accoutrements, etc. I sold by auction with the assistance of a sergeant, whom I appointed auctioneer, and transmitted the amount generated – deducting the expenses – to the adjutant of the regiment.

Next day, I called on an old friend of mine who was a subaltern in the 97th, whose name was William Dowman, whose right arm had been amputated. One morning when they were besieging Badajoz, he had retired in the company of Captain Coppinger, in command of a fatigue company, to take a little refreshment: this generally consists of either cows'

---

21   Apparently not that situated within the walls in the upper town, which has been restored recently.

tongue, heart, or kidneys: the regimental butchers claim these as their perquisite, which they usually dispose of to the officers, two shillings being the price of the former, and 18 pence each for the latter.

They selected what they thought was a snug retreat under a hillock 5 or 6 feet high, but a few minutes after they had been seated a shell from the town passed over it and dropped between them and exploded; one part hit Dowman's right arm and made a sponge of it (as I don't suppose a bone of it longer than my finger survived between his wrist and shoulder). Coppinger had a small share of it, for a piece about the size of the ball of one's hand but not so thick, which he afterwards picked up, hit his legs and took the calves completely away, leaving the sinews or muscles exposed, quite in strings, dangling in different lengths. Both Dowman and Coppinger were placed on a car and brought into Elvas. When the former was operated on, he apparently bore it with great fortitude, and never complained during the time they took off his arm; and when the doctor had dressed it, he immediately fell soundly asleep for twelve hours. I called on him the following morning, when he told me that he scarcely felt it. He lived about ten days, after which mortification took place, and he departed.[22] In these hot countries, those who are wounded are too often fatally so.

22   Ensign William Dowman died of his wounds on 4 June.

CHAPTER 11

Frustrated at Badajoz; and Retirement

ON THE MORNING OF 3 June, our artillery, securely positioned, commenced their second bombardment of Badajoz, which they continued for several days with some success. On the 8th, at 1 o'clock on the morning, a party under the command of a field officer from the Light Brigade attempted to escalade the walls of Fort San Cristóbal, but ineffectually, partly due to miscalculations, the scaling ladders having been made several feet too short, the highest rungs not even reaching the top of the wall. The commander,[1] together with five commissioned officers and eighty rank and file, were killed or wounded. If they had taken possession of the fort, this would have greatly accelerated the outcome of the siege.

However, the guns on the other side of the town were not idle, continuing to fire with increased energy on that day and the next; but the number of wounded increased so rapidly that Elvas could not contain them: already there were some 5,000 British alone there. As there was no room for more, many were forwarded to Estremoz, about two and a half leagues further west.

Another attempt was made to take San Cristóbal on the evening of the 10th, but the fort was not to fall, the garrison being continuously on the alert since the first attack; and on

---

1   Major Aeneas Mackintosh, 85th Foot.

*Map 3: A French plan of Badajoz, with Fort San Cristóbal
on the north bank of the Guadiana*

this occasion our men could not even reach the foot of the walls, and 200 were killed or wounded before they retired.[2] To take one of these forts by escalade is no joke. However, bombardment of the town continued without intermission on the 11th and 12th, though without having any serious effect on the garrison.

On the morning of the 13th, the Commander-in-Chief gave orders for two divisions – the 3rd and 7th – to raise the siege, quit Badajoz, and join the other divisions which were encamped to the north-east; and that the 2nd and 4th, which were in advance, were to follow them. These four British divisions, consisting of 80,000 men, thus bivouacked between Arronches to the north-west, Campo Maior on the north-east, and Elvas to the south-east. It was said that this was in expectation that Marshal Soult, commonly referred to as the Duke of Dalmatia,[3] who had received strong reinforcements, would be returning to provoke another engagement. But his Lordship was not unprepared, having concentrated his strength and leaving himself room to manoeuvre. Nevertheless, it was risky to leave so many of the sick and disabled so far in advance, even briefly, despite having troops at hand to protect them while being conveyed back from Elvas to the Depot at Belém.

Elvas was extraordinarily busy now, as a General Order had been issued that everyone intending to remain in the town should provide themselves with six months' provisions, as it was likely that the French would attack it. Our medical department was active in the removal of the wounded, and

---

2   This is an exaggeration: Oman lists 54 killed, 81 wounded, and 4 missing: 130 in total.

3   Marshal [Nicolas] Jean-de-Dieu Soult, Duc de Dalmatie (1769–1851), who was long Wellington's redoubtable opponent, notably during the last nine months of the war.

1. *Officer and private of the 27th Regiment (Inniskillings) in 1815, by P.W. Reynolds. They are both from the 'Light' Company, displaying green plumes and hunting horns on their shakos, and 'wings' on their shoulders. The officer wears a scarlet jacket and crimson sash, gold epaulettes, and carries a light cavalry sabre (those of other companies had a straight sword). The private, handling an Indian pattern 'Brown Bess' musket, wears a brick-red jacket: facings were buff. This drawing will display slight differences in uniform to that worn in 1811, which, by the time it had seen much service in the Peninsula, would have looked very different: sun-faded, tattered and patched, and shakos shapeless . . .*

2. *Recruiting scene, but for the 33rd Regiment, by George Walker (1781–1856).*

3. *View of Ballyshannon from the east, with the salmon leap in the foreground, by Thomas Roberts (1748–77).*

4. *View of the Cove of Cork in 1811, by Nicholas Pocock (1741–1821).*

5. *Troops embarking at Cobh (detail), by John Nixon (1760–1818).*

6. *View of Lisbon in the autumn of 1808, with the aqueduct of Alcântara, by the Revd William Bradford (1780–1857).*

7. The west front of Convent of Mafra, by an unknown artist.

8. Santarém, as seen from a British advance post, with the Tagus on the right, published by Edward Orme.

9 The advance on Pombal, left burning by Maséna's troops, 11 March 1811, by Major Thomas Staunton St Clair (1785–1847).

10. The Río Guadiana seen from Juromenha.

11. View of Elvas from the north, with the Forte de Graça in the foreground, with the Amoreira aqueduct to the right, published by Edward Orme.

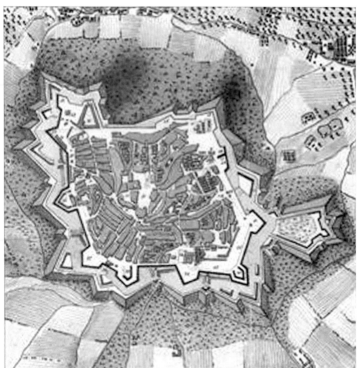

12. A Portuguese plan of Elvas in 1802. The bastion at the top right faces due north; the Amoreira aqueduct enters the town just south of the north-western bastions.

13. 'Johnny on the Sick List', from The Military Adventures of Johnny Newcombe, by Thomas Rowlandson (1756–1827).

14. 'Portsmouth Point', by Thomas Rowlandson (1756–1827).

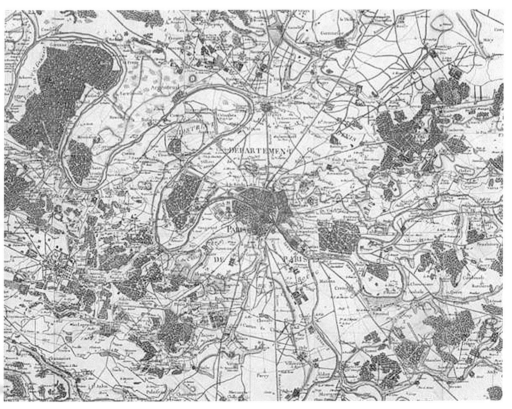

15. Detail from Cassini's Map of Paris and its environs.

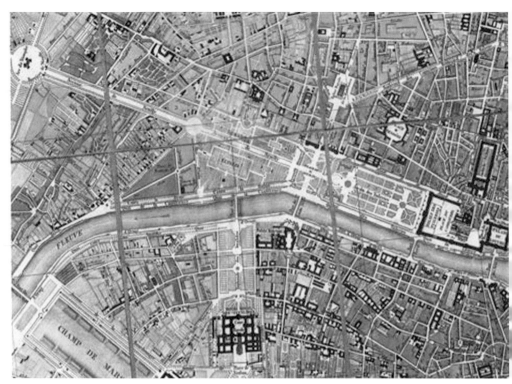

16. *Detail of a plan of Paris by X. Girard, 1826. The Arc de Triomphe is seen top left; the Palais Royal at right centre (east of the Place Vendôme), with the Palais des Tuileries and Palais du Louvre below; Les Invalides is at lower centre; the Pont d'Iéna by the left margin.*

17. *The courtyard of the Château de Neuilly, by Jacques Swebach (1769–1823).*

18. *British encampment in the Bois de Boulogne, by Lieutenant George Scharf (1788–1860).*

19. *Allied troops cantoned in the environs of Paris, July 1815, by Etienne-Jean Delécluze (1781–1863).*

20. *The Tuileries from the Quai d'Orsay in 1814, with a distant view of the hill of Montmartre, by Etienne Bouhot (1780–1862).*

21. The principal entrance to the Musée Royal in the Louvre in about 1822, by Etienne Bouhot (1780–1862).

22. The Place Vendôme in 1808, by Etienne Bouhot (1780–1862).

23. Femmes légères *soliciting in the galleries of the Palais Royal, by Louis-Léopold Boilly (1761–1845), from a sketch of 1804.*

24. *Wellington's Headquarters in Paris, detail, by Pierre-Gabriel Berthault.*

25. *The Pavillon de Valois of the Château de St Cloud, by Siméon Fort (1793–1861).*

26. *The Bakewell family tombs in the churchyard of St Edward, King and Martyr, Castle Donington; Robert Bakewell lies in the central table tomb.*

27. *An anonymous portrait of Robert Bakewell in middle age.*

great credit is due to its staff stationed there, for we never had need to make application to them a second time, be the case be ever so urgent; but I suspect their conduct on this occasion was an exception to the general rule, for as a body they were rather awkward and callous characters.

By chance, about a week before the alarm was given, I went into one of the many convents converted into hospitals, and saw a bunch of those medical men assembled. I was told that they were discussing what limbs required amputation. I waited around, and saw them take off eleven legs, and – for the first time in my life – I began to feel as if I would faint; and it was with difficulty that I kept on my legs until reaching the foot of the stairs, when, with a little fresh air, I recovered myself.

I found that all these operations, even the most desperate, were performed by one of the most experienced professional surgeons amongst them, but not without the assistance and advice of others of their fraternity: on that day he personally amputated scores of limbs, including legs and arms, and they were removed expeditiously.

It was astonishing to see the speed and dispatch with which the town was cleared of such numbers of maimed and crippled men, three hundred of whom were my responsibility as belonging to the 27th Regiment. On their arrival in Belém, they came under the control of Captain Archibald Mair. There were seldom ever less than 10,000 men in this general Depot, established there as being the only place near the mouth of the Tagus large enough not only to accommodate them, and also being convenient for their embarkation.

Once the greater part of the wounded had been removed, the officers stationed in Elvas asked permission to rejoin their respective regiments, so the Commander applied to Headquarters for instructions. We waited for several days, after which, as no answer was forthcoming, the request was repeated, but still without eliciting any reply. So we hung about here until the morning of 22 June, by which time all the wounded and sick were evacuated, apart from a very few, only just alive and unsafe to move, who were left unprotected in one of the convents.

The inhabitants had been busy during the last few days in storing enough provisions for six months, but the British officers did not think it necessary, until we saw two French cavalry regiments which had crossed the Guadiana, rapidly approaching. At this, our 11th Regiment of Light Dragoons, stationed about two miles from the walls, having taken up a favourable position, bore down on them in great style, broke their line, and put them in confusion. Many were wounded, and a number of prisoners taken. It is astonishing to see how active our Light Cavalry are, a most useful force in this countryside which, being quite open, gives them a fine field for their exertions; and, in general, they are much better mounted than the cavalry of any other nation. In this action – very plainly seen from the walls of Elvas – our 11th Regiment did as well as had the 13th at Campo Maior, or at least as much or more than was expected they could.

The gates of Elvas were closed soon after the commencement of this action. We were all a bustle, for – orders or no orders – it would not do to be penned in the town without provisions, and we lost no time in preparing to leave. My servant and I had my baggage packed and loaded, and the horse outside the walls before the third pair of gates was closed. I thought it unusual that so many officers should have been left in Elvas without orders from the fountain head; and quitting the place on their own responsibility. But, having cleared the gates, we were uncertain whether to turn right or left, until my servant, understanding the language, heard from a *paisano* where or troops were, so we steered in that direction. After a mile, we met a detachment of the 11th Light Dragoons escorting two French officers and some twenty prisoners, beyond which we continued for about two and a half leagues without any check, to find the 27th bivouacked with the rest of the division in fields at Torre de Mora,[4] the whole army being dispersed thereabouts.

On the following day I rode around the camp, where the 1st, 2nd, 3rd, 6th, 7th, and the Light Divisions were assembled, their united strength presumably being more than sufficient to thwart any hostile thrust that the enemy might attempt to make in this quarter and, at the same time, to cover the removal of the disabled to Belém.

On my return, Lieutenant Philip Gordon,[5] commanding the 8th company, asked me to join them, as he had lost two subalterns, but our commanding officer wanted me with the 2nd, to which I had been attached before, and where I found only one officer remaining, for Captain William Dobbin, who had formerly commanded it, had volunteered for the Portuguese service and had joined one of their regiments of *caçadores*. Lieutenant Frederick Harding,[6] who had remained with it, was a bad mathematician, and could not keep his accounts on any order, due to the casualties suffered by the company during recent weeks; thus the pay of the company devolved on me, who found a deficit of 40 dollars in my receipts from what the men claimed from the balance sheets, which proved to have originated when Captain Dobbin passed over the accounts to Harding.

Our Light Dragoons in advance of Elvas compelled the French cavalry to re-cross the Guadiana with considerable loss. However restless the French appeared to be on far bank of the river, they thought it more politic to remain there, as being the best side of

---

4   Unlocated.
5   He was mortally wounded at Vitoria.
6   He was to be killed at the storming of San Sebastian.

the hedge from which to run, which allowed the gates of Elvas to be reopened and our communication with it resumed.

That all our wounded had reached their destination safely was the reason given for an inspection of the right brigade of the 4th Division by General Cole on Friday 12 July. Due to our losses at Badajoz and Albuera, some additional regiments were added to the division, which then was made up as follow: the right brigade: the 27th, 40th, and 97th; the right centre brigade by the 1st Portuguese Lusitanian and the 11th and 23rd Portuguese regiments; the left centre brigade by the 5th Portuguese *Caçadores*, and the 13th Portuguese regiment; the left brigade consisted of the British 7th, 23rd, and 48th.

The right brigade marched one league to a convenient ground for its inspection, and our general complimented them on their strict discipline in going through their different manoeuvres, after which they returned to their encampment, reached at about 5.0. I then visited the 48th Regiment, where I found Captain William Chesslyn[7] enjoying a glass of wine and a cigar. He probed about 5 inches into the ground (where they are often placed to keep them moist), pulled out a bundle and passed me one, and I spent that rest of the evening with him.

The following morning (Saturday 13 July) three divisions were ordered out to be inspected by Lord Wellington: the 2nd and 4th, together with General Hamilton's Light Division.[8] We reached the ground at the appointed time, and in our wake rode my Lord Wellington accompanied by the Prince of Orange and other nobility,[9] together with a large retinue from the three

---

7   He was severely wounded at Salamanca.

8   Sir John Hamilton (1755–1835).

9   Prince William of Orange (1792–1847), a well-liked youth who, although inexperienced, commanded an Allied Corps in the Waterloo Campaign, and became William II of the Netherlands in 1840.

kingdoms: British, Portuguese, and Spanish. When he orders an inspection, it is a generally assumed that an engagement is expected to take place before long; and the reason for ordering the divisions out alternately was to ascertain the actual strength on which he might depend if required to take the field. It was a fine day, but they are all fine days at this season; and each division went through its customary manoeuvres and received the usual compliments.

Next day, being Sunday, and being paraded on that account, our divisional clergyman (the Revd George Jenkins) delivered Protestant prayers at the drum head, though the usual church service was much abridged. Occasionally, he adds a sermon at the conclusion.

The weather is extremely hot, and a report was spread, that contrary to our expectations, the French had ordered their army into cantonments, which was the reason why our division left the fields of Torre de Mora on the evening of the 21st to bivouac in those of Borba.[10]

---

10   Borba is a small town with marble quarries some 18 miles west of Elvas, on the road to Estremoz.

CHAPTER 12

Estremoz; and Illness

EARLY ON 23 JULY WE continued our march, reaching Estremoz by 11.0, where we cantoned, the heat by then being almost unsupportable.[1] Here, I obtained a billet on a respectable tradesman, who was most hospitable. Sometimes I used to go to church with the family, and when I did so they were kind to a degree: I could not please them more than by attending mass, which I did on my first full day there. The church was open every day, but only one or two of their Catholic priests are usually in attendance, although there are frequently several of them performing rites in some of the larger churches, penned up in a separate section to carry out their duties to their distinct congregations.

At 10.0 I attended parade; and at 11.0 my landlord came to tell me that he had locked the door, would be closing the shutters, and wished me to roost, as he and all his family were going to bed, which they did, and slept until 3.30. This is their custom throughout the Summer, their shops being closed from 11.0 until 4.0, when business is recommenced.[2] That evening, I promenaded with the family until almost 10.0, when we

---

1   This is confirmed among others by William Tomkinson, who wrote on 18 July that the weather was 'dreadfully hot, and the army very sickly; they say more than 20,000 in hospital.'

2   Bakewell writes that he then 'took a lounge for these five hours, when I returned and took my dinner', but whether he went out for a saunter or stayed in for a nap, is unclear!

retired. The Portuguese rise early, due to them having dozed away a greater part of the preceding day.

The religious buildings throughout both Portugal and Spain are very grand,[3] and these peoples are great devotees, being prejudiced in favour of their system of superstitious idolatry, and I believe all of them to be Roman Catholics, as I never met with an exception. They would appear to spare no expense to ornament their places of worship, which are decorated with all the finery one can imagine; and, with a few exceptions, these churches are attached to a convent, some being as much as three to five storeys high, in which the friars — who appear to be the drudges of the priesthood — live much on the same system as in our barracks: but not all are so large.

In Portugal, they never bury their dead in coffins. The survivors of the departed apply to the priest, and when a day and hour for the interment is fixed, a detachment of friars is ordered to have everything in readiness; firstly the grave, which is dug very deep. In this, the corpses are placed one above the other until they reach one foot from the top, when it is closed. A number of friars (depending on the credit of the family concerned) leave the church at say half an hour before the burial, four or six of them carrying a kind of bier on their shoulders, similar to a small hearse except that it opens on the side instead of at the end, and bears plumes. The friars sing all the way to the house of the deceased, being only silent while the body (usually wrapped in a kind of flannel or linen) makes its appearance and is placed in the bier. The chant then recommences as they proceed to the place of burial, where a priest is waiting to perform a ceremony lasting about fifteen

---

3   Having hardly set foot in a single Spanish town of any consequence other than Olivenza, one must assume that Bakewell's knowledge of its churches was only at second-hand.

minutes, at which, other than members of the family or close friends, few attend. The body is then taken from the bier and placed in the grave – perhaps upon half a dozen others, depending. These priests and friars – particularly those belonging to one of the larger establishments – are supported by the income received from their extensive properties, but the Portuguese are apparently so devoted to their clergy, that I don't suppose they would complain even if three parts of the country's revenue went to subsidise their maintenance.

These convents and churches were frequently served as barracks on our marches; but at Elvas they were more serviceable as hospitals, with no less than seven of them being appropriated for the wounded, etc.

On 25 July a fair was held in Estremoz – the first I had seen in Portugal – attended by crowds dressed in their best clothes, some to see, others to be seen. They are similar to those in England, except that their merchandise and produce are very different. Jewellery appeared to be the staple commodity, stalls of which were aligned for almost a mile, loaded with an assortment of trinkets, gold, silverware, and enamelled work of striking diversity.

There was an abundance of fruit for sale also, such as oranges, plums, apricots, peaches, melons, apricots, lemons, nectarines, apples, pears, walnuts, figs, nuts and almonds; but the grapes were not yet ripe, or there would have been plenty. The orchards are heavy with these different fruits. Oranges and lemons seem to be in season throughout the year, not dropping when ripe, but continue to hang until the succeeding crop is ready.

A great number of horses and mules were for sale; only a scattering of cows, but no sheep: indeed, I saw only one flock in Portugal, and that was at Elvas, and they were kept for milking, as English farmers would have dairy cows. I can only assume that the army had already cleared the country of sheep, for they were reputed for the superior quality of their wool and mutton, and flocks and herds used to be numerous also.

The weather was now extremely hot, making it virtually impossible at that time of year for armies to support the long and fatiguing marches they had undertaken at the commencement of the campaign without the danger of numbers of men falling ill. Our officers expected that we would be stationed here for some time, although Portugal was now largely free of the French; and a battle at this season would be attended by destructive consequences, as the intense heat would cause mortification to take place in a high proportion of wounds. But this was not the only reason for our general's apparent inactivity: of more relevance was the fact that powerful reinforcements were expected from England at any day.

Meanwhile, on 30 July, it was resolved by the majority of our officers that a sergeant should be sent to Lisbon forthwith to collect the plate belonging to their mess, which they had decided to form at Estremoz. However, hardly more than two hours after his departure, orders were received for the 4th Division to be in readiness to march north at 1 o'clock next morning. Our destination would be almost 200 miles away, for it was considered pretty certain that the French, under Marmont's command,[4] were preparing to attack those units of our army remaining there while a much higher proportion of the total was facing Soult's forces in the south.[5]

---

4   Marshal Auguste Frédéric Marmont, Duc de Raguse (1774–1852), a good strategist, who replaced Masséna after Fuentes de Oñoro. He was seriously wounded at Salamanca.

5   Welington had left Sir Brent Spencer with the 1st, 5th, 6th, and Light Divisions; and two Portuguese infantry brigades, plus cavalry: altogether some 26,000 foot and 1,800 horse, to watch that sector of the frontier.

So, at 4.0 in the morning of 31 July, at least 30,000 men started their march north from Estremoz for Castelo Branco and Ciudad Rodrigo, firstly to Fronteira, where we bivouacked that evening; and at 2.0 next morning we left for Crato, five long leagues distance on a scorching day, and the roads so dusty that we were frequently up to our knees in it. Because of this, throughout our march, guards were placed round every pond and dirty puddle to prevent the men from making themselves ill by drinking the filthy water. It was a critical day for our troops, due to the intolerable heat and their excessive fatigue. We slept at Crato and set out for Alpalhão at 2.0. By leaving our roost so early we were able to accomplish the greater part of the day's march before the sun exercised its full force.[6]

On the morning of 3 August we left Alpalhão at the usual hour for Nisa, and never was I drier than at my arrival there, when I immediately went and bought two bottles of Lisbon wine and drank the lot at almost one draught.[7]

The 4th Division halted at Nisa all next day before leaving for Castelo Branco,[8] but there was no chance of me accompany them, having been attacked meanwhile with a complaint which they call the cholera morbus.[9] This was exasperating, as at this time I both commanded and paid the 21st company; but the severity of the disorder quite disabled

---

6   The effects of dehydration on the troops in the Peninsula have not yet been given due attention.

7   By 'Lisbon' wine, Bakewell may well have meant that of Carcavelos.

8   Nisa was a small town on the road some ten miles south of the main crossing-point of the Tagus in Portugal at Vila Velha de Ródão, beyond which the road veered north-east via Castelo Branco towards the frontier area between Almeida and Ciudad Rodrigo.

9   Now referred to as acute gastroenteritis, this was usually caused by eating or drinking contaminated food or water, the symptoms being diarrhoea and vomiting, and resulting in dehydration.

me, just when I flattered myself of being in a position to gain some promotion, and as this was the only instance I had ever being ill since infancy (except for very occasional and temporary cases, caused my own irregularities): indeed it was most unfortunate.

I suffered greatly on the 6th and 7th and, on the following two days, was continually evacuating both in front and rear, which much weakened me; and intermittently during the next few, blood would pour from my nostrils, which together with everything else, caused great debility; and yet I believe that in this case the flow from my nose was the main reason for my survival. A surgeon from the 2nd Division attended me, a Mr N —— , but with very little effect; and as I was seized by the ague every other day and occasionally by a stronger fever,[10] I was anxious to reach Lisbon as soon as possible; but how to get there was the problem, for I could then hardly stand on my feet.

Fortunately, on my eighth day at Nisa, there came a few commissary wagons of the 27th, each drawn by eight horses, on their way to Abrantes, on one of which I asked to be conveyed. Meanwhile, as a young woman belonging to the 97th Regiment offered her services, I agreed to take her with me, thinking she might serve as nurse. In the circumstances, it seemed sensible to send my servant with my horse to Lisbon – but by a different and more direct route – so that he might find a good billet by the time I arrived.

On the following day, my baggage previously loaded, I left for Abrantes in one of those wagons, accompanied by my nurse and two others passengers. This was a two-day stage, but I was too incapacitated to take much notice of the places we traversed. On the second day, the unevenness of the road

---

10   Ague usually refers to malarial fever.

caused the wagon to overturn, luckily without injuring anyone; but its contents were pitched out, and I lost my gun.[11]

That evening we reached Abrantes, below which flowed the Tagus, to find boats for Lisbon waiting to take us on board; but due to my weakness, when I was attempting to get into one of them, I fell on its edge, causing a severe contusion; indeed, I thought it likely that I had broken a rib. It was a three-day sail, delayed on the second by our boat running aground. By then, I was quite unable to stand, and feeling my life in danger and in need of advice and support, I asked some men of our escort to carry me to the local governor's house, lie me on the floor, and stay with me until he had provided us with a passage on another vessel, ours now being stuck fast. At first, swearing, he refused; but, not wanting so many unwelcome guests, had found another within hours, to which I was carried, and we set sail again, disembarking next day at Lisbon.

My servant was waiting for me, having found a billet at 57 Travessa dos Fiéis de Deus.[12] While he went to fetch a cart, I was carried into the Commissary's warehouse, where one of the clerks gave me some mulled wine and dry toast, which much restored me, having had nothing but tea to drink since leaving Nisa. After an hour, my servant arrived to take me and the luggage to my lodgings, where I slept very soundly.

Next morning, I sent a message to Mr Hogg, the Deputy Inspector of Hospitals, asking him for some medical assistance, which he sent that same day, and attended by a staff surgeon (who was of great service) I gradually improved. By 31 August I was able to go to a church, but I'd never seen one as full, for the

---

11   We are not told of what type, although Bakewell says it was his favourite, being ornamented, and had belonged to a Spanish officer formerly.

12   This alley survives in the Bairro Alto.

priest was an extempore preacher, the first I had heard of since my arrival in the Peninsula.

I will now expatiate on the curiosities of this city: for nothing was more gratifying than to observe the customs and habits of this volatile people. Their coffee-houses seem to hold a great share of the youth and beauty of both sexes, who congregate in them day and night, from which, when paired off, they go to bagnios,[13] where hot baths are provided, into which these couples plunge and stay 'until their voluptuous and amorous customs are cloyed.'

Lisbon is also notable for both its jewellers and fruiterers shops, the latter for the variety, size, and delicious flavour of their fruit, equalling if not excelling those of other countries; and providence has so arranged that the grape should be at their perfection at the time when most needed, when the heat is almost unbearable; and there is also a deal of nutriment in the grape.

At night the citizens are annoyed by both lizards and mosquitoes; the former, though harmless and inoffensive, are unpleasant little reptiles, similar to a rat and of a greenish colour, and frequently criss-crossed one's bed. At first, I wondered how they got in. If you sleep in the first floor, they are sure to visit you, and these nocturnal wanderers pay their respects to you repeatedly whether on the second, third, or fourth floors; but this was accounted for after inspecting the partitions, in which the wainscotings provided a safe retreat in which to proliferate.

The mosquitoes are a kind of large fly which make a great humming noise during the night, and bite very freely. The

---

13   A bagnio, originally a Turkish coffee-house offering the facility of baths, by the mid eighteenth century was a euphemism for a brothel, or at least a house in which a room could be hired, no questions asked.

lizards, mosquitoes, and the smaller insects are the most troublesome visitors; but when we slept in the fields, snakes and scorpions were what we particularly had to guard against: they were not very common, and yet I have seen them occasionally. Before we lay down, our servants used to clear the ground for a few yards around us, taking away the stones, etc.

The buildings in Lisbon are generally four or five storeys high, but are lighter, less solid and substantial than the English, having no brick or stone except a little of the latter in their foundations; but they seem to be both cosy and airy, more suited to their hot climate and more fancifully ornamented than ours. Timber and plaster are the principal materials used in their erection, and they are occasionally washed or stuccoed, depending on their owner's taste. They often have balconies along their fronts, which appear to run from one end of a street to the other.

The inhabitants of Lisbon still continue that filthy custom of emptying their chamber-pots into the street, as no necessaries are built for their convenience. One day, I accidentally opened one of the bedroom doors at my billet, to find my landlord doing his duty in a pot in one corner, and his wife was doing hers in another vessel in the opposite one! These, when full, are usually placed in their attics until the evening, and at 11 o'clock they start to pour out their contents, to free them for use the following day. From 11.0 until 1.0 every night, the metropolis is continuously receiving these 'honey drops' from the upper balconies. Families, if visiting their neighbours, usually avoid those hours, for should they be out in the streets at that time, in all probability their clothes will receive a shower of dung.

My surgeon recommended that I be examined by a Medical Board. These are held twice a month to hear complaints and to decide what action should be taken, depending on the condition of each sick and wounded officer. On 5 September

I attended one, when Dr McDougall was President, while two other doctors constituted the board. I had come across him frequently when on duty at Elvas, and he recognised me, despite my greatly reduced state. The following is a copy of the order I received from the board:

> Lisbon, September 11, 1811
> Proceedings of a medical board held by order of Ab Bolton, Esqr. Deputy Inspector of Hospitals in compliance with the general orders dated Cartaxo, February 5, 1811.
>
> President, Dr McDougle [sic]: Members, William Richard Morel,[14] & William Corke
>
> The board having met and minutely examined into the state of health of Ensign Bakewell of the 27th Regiment, find that he is severely affected with intermittent fever, which has reduced him to a degree of extreme debility, and recommend that he should be allowed to return to England for the reestablishment of his health.

A true copy	Signed: McDougle
Robert Atkinson	Wm. Rcad. Morel
J.G.	Wm. Corke

On receiving this, I made application to Captain Mair, the officer in command of the 27th at the Depot, for an advance of pay due to my expected departure; and he gave me two months'. I also forwarded to Lieutenant Maclean the book containing the accounts and balance due to and from the men of the 21st company, whose settlements the adjutant acknowledged prior

---

14   Probably he was Staff Surgeon William Richard Morell.

to me receiving my final orders some days later. The following is a copy:

> Extract from General Orders, Adjutant General's office, Fuenteguinaldo,
> 12 September 1811
>
> Mem. II   The following officers have received the Commander of the Forces leave of absence for the recovery of health:
> Ensign Bakewell, 27th Regiment, 2 months England.

True copy	Signed:
G. Darrol Cole	C. Stewart

CHAPTER 13

Transported Home

ON 17 SEPTEMBER I RECEIVED my Leave of Absence for two months from Headquarters, and as Lieutenant Simpson[1] had received his on the same day for the same length of time, we agreed to return together, both being in the same regiment, and immediately set about laying in our sea stock. Next day, I went on board the *Mariner* transport, Captain John Patterson, carrying eight guns and rated for 350 tons, where I secured my passage.

We set sail from the Tagus on the 19th, but regrettably, due to some misunderstanding between myself and Simpson, I found that he had boarded a different transport. The officers sailing with me were Lieutenants Bell of the 95th, McCrea of the 13th Light Dragoons, Langstaff of the 71st, and Ensign Cooke of the 9th.

The provisions I had accumulated were 1 dozen each of Port and Lisbon wine, which cost me 15/-; 1 lb of tea; ½ stone of sugar; and a few chickens, with a supply of bread, butter, and biscuits, and a quantity of sago, as the latter was strongly recommended to me, and on which I principally subsisted. We cleared the harbour under the protection of the 38-gun frigate HMS *Melpomene*,[2] in a convoy of twenty-nine other ships.

Unfortunately, on the first evening out, we found that we had a very troublesome cabin passenger with us: McCrea

---

1   Formerly Ensign William Simpson.
2   This frigate had been captured by Admiral Hood at Calvi in 1794.

appeared to be deranged, and for no other reason except for the loss of his baggage, which was apparently very valuable, as including a deal of jewellery and money; and this preyed on his mind; nor had he any clothes except what he wore. At about 1 o'clock at night, he arose from his hammock and went to that of Lieutenant Bell's, where, taking hold of his head, he began to shake him. Bell extricated himself and thought he had got clear; but after a time, McCrea got up again and began to make water on the berths in which each officer was roosting. Without Bell realising it, McCrea had also grabbed his clothes, put them on, and thus wandered up and down different parts of the vessel until daylight. When Bell awoke, much to his annoyance (for they were new) he couldn't find his uniform, at least not until discovered by Langstaff, although by then hardly recognizable. McCrea, who was on deck, had still got them on, but having rolled in all the pitch, tar, and filth he could find, they were completely ruined. When Bell and I accosted him and demanded their return, he began to whistle and kick, athough this didn't hurt as he was bare footed. We went to complain to Captain Patterson, insisting that he provide separate berths for either us or the madman. And so McCrea was confined in a small room adjoining our cabin, where he remained locked in night and day, except when his servant gave him food: whistling, laughing, and singing was all he did during the rest of the voyage.

All the officers on board were returning home as being too disabled either by wounds or sickness to carry out their duties: both Bell and Langstaff were wounded, while both Cooke and I were incapacitated by the same complaint.[3] As the ague often visited us, we used to lie in our berths most of the day and

3   None of these officers are listed among the physically wounded in John Hall's *Biographical Dictionary*.

night; and there we just roosted, wagging our chins at each other to the no small amusement of our comrades.

The wind being unfavourable on the 20th, we made little progress due to so much tacking to and fro; and I experienced on this voyage what I had never seen or heard of before, what is called a break of the sea.[4]

The officers' cabins were at the stern of the ship. I was half asleep or dozing at about 10.0 in the morning, when we were violently jolted, and heard a sudden and tremendous crash, almost as if in our room. We all immediately jumped out of our berths only to plunge up to our waists in water. Not having the slightest idea of what had happened, I assumed it was all over with us and that we were going to the bottom; but as the others were scrambling to get on deck, I quickly followed. To my surprise, we learnt that no danger was envisaged, and that the only damage we had sustained was the loss of two pigs swept off by the sea, together with a few other trifling articles on deck. But on returning to our cabin, what a smash-up presented itself. There was not a single pane left in the stern windows, nor a single frame in place, except for a few detached pieces: both the wood and glass were smashed to atoms. We had to put up shutters – what the sailors term dead-lights – to prevent the wind and rain beating in, except for a little peep-hole left to give us some light.

On the following Thursday the wind was more favourable, and continued so until 4 October, during which time we sailed along at 5 to 8 knots an hour, bringing us near the English Channel, which our captain said he would attempt to enter next morning. In the event, he was unsuccessful, due, so he said, to the tempestuous and boisterous weather, and the very

---

4   These are rogue or freak waves spontaneously produced in mid-ocean, which frequently rise to well in excess of 25 metres.

strong wind. As the whole of the convoy except the *Mariner* was able to make a clear course into the Channel, I justifiably suspected that Langstaff, who had been on deck with Captain Patterson the previous night, had bribed him to steer for the Cove of Cork; and this at the request of Ensign Cooke, who came from County Athlone, and who was so very ill that he hardly expected to reach home alive. On voicing our suspicions, the captain said he would have another go, and we saw that he tried three times to do so, almost dashing the vessel against the Rocks of Scilly, avoided by a few yards only. On his last attempt, we actually scraped against something which, as he admitted, was such a hazard that he would rather bear out to sea until the storm had abated. Despite this, Bell and I found it very hard to understand why Patterson had apparently been unable to enter the Channel unless he was bribed, for we knew that Cooke had a long purse. However, as he continued to exaggerate the danger, and we were the only two Englishmen among the passengers, we were overruled.

On the morning of 6 October, on being warned that a French privateer had been sighted, and might attack, I went on deck to see her circling around us, but at a respectable distance. She had hoisted American colours, but nevertheless appeared to be making hostile preparations. Our sailors were already at their guns, and the captain started to distribute cutlasses, blunderbusses and pistols. The few prisoners sailing with us were ordered below and placed in a cabin under guard; and how they laugh and jabbered away in French at the prospect of being rescued, when they would take their revenge on our crew; but providence provided otherwise. However, while we paced the deck with the captain – cutlasses in hand and pistols in our belts – the privateer decided to sheer off, having skimming around us three or four times just out of reach of our guns, but we had been unable to ascertain precisely whence she came or was bound. Our transport was a great lumbering vessel (rated at 350 tons only, but more likely 500) and she carried only eight guns, though pierced for over twice the number; so we attributed our safety to our unwieldy size; for if that privateer had attacked us seriously, we must have surrendered in the end.

The storm continued, with our captain still keeping well clear of the coast, until the next morning, when we were again roused from our slumber, for another ship hove in sight, and the same defensive preparations were made; but it never came near enough for us to make out her strength or description, and soon disappeared. We kept on rolling about until the 9th, when, after the storm, came a calm, and all was quite still and clear. The captain now brought out his chart, checked our position, and informed us that we were only fifty miles from the Cove of Cork, to which it would be wise to steer; and there we dropped anchor next day, 10 October.

On landing, Langstaff set out for Belfast post haste. Cooke's friends were sent to collect him (for he was in no state to travel alone to Athlone), only to arrive a few hours before he died. He was a genteel, promising youth just short of twenty-one, at which age, had he lived, he would have taken possession of an estate of several hundred pounds a year.

Whether our captain was actually driven from the English Channel due to the weather, or been tempted by the Irishman's purse, we could never be certain; but if the latter, his conduct was indeed answerable, for he had nearly found himself in a French port, which happened to an English brig, the *Portuense*, only a few days afterwards. It had met the same privateer that had annoyed us on the 6th, and taken into harbour on the 15th, when the French crew acknowledged their error in not persevering in their attack on us.

But errors are frequently committed by the most enlightened; and it was certainly a very grave one to hazard the lives of so many officers returning to England in convoy, and without medical attention on board; for Ensign Cooke's death was caused by lack of such, and doubtless many others have expired due to similar negligence.

After making repeated applications for transfer, Lieutenant Bell and I boarded the *Reward*, Robert Rochester, Master, which was bound for Portsmouth in company with fourteen other vessels packed with Irish Militia and detachments from the 6th and 71st regiments.

We had not been long afloat when a boat came alongside with an officer who wished to embark. Luckily, we recognized McCrea and, after some discussion, were able to prevent him; and whistling away as he had come, he drew away. Bell had been in Cork on the previous day to visit an officer of the 95th on recruiting service there, who had provided him with a complete outfit of regimentals. With reason, Bell was scared that McCrea might attempt to repeat his frolic had he been permitted aboard.

While at the Cove, we slept on the ship, but dined and breakfasted at the coffee house on the beach most days. Other officers who joined us on the *Reward* were Lieutenants Roberts of the 71st Regiment,[5] and Nightingale, together with his brother, an Ensign, both in the 6th, and Sherlock of the Carlow Militia. They had been placed in command of separate detachments of their respective regiments already on board, waiting for a favourable wind to take us to Portsmouth. Our fleet set sail on 18 October, but due to a contrary wind we were unable to clear the harbour.

---

5   Bakewell had noted that this Roberts was a son of a gentleman of that name who was a banker at Cork; and that this youth had stripped and jumped from the vessel into the sea, when the waves were rolling high, but was saved by clinging to the captain's boat.

An unfortunate accident occurred that day, when a private of the Carlow Militia attempting to come aboard, slipped and fell into the sea; he swam for about a minute in the sight of us all, and sank to rise no more.

At some time during the night of the 19th, a man of the 6th Regiment was detected cutting the ship's cable, but he was seized before completing the mischief and placed in confinement, where he will stay until a Court Martial is held to try him.

The wind remained unfavourable until the 27th, when, belatedly, we were able to get away. It was a tolerable passage, but certainly not a very rapid one, for we did not make Portsmouth until 1 November.

Here I disembarked, dined, and took coach for London, reached the following morning. It had taken precisely six weeks to travel from Lisbon to Portsmouth, thirteen days of which were from Cork to Portsmouth.

CHAPTER 14

Castle Donington

DURING MY STAY IN LONDON, where I remained until the 6th, I called on the Colonel (the Earl of Moira), and likewise on our agent, Mr Ridge,[1] and drew a little necessary cash to enable me to proceed home. I also went to see Dr Weir, the President of the Board, who sat at certain hours each day to examine wounded or disabled officers, and he didn't hesitate a minute to provide me with a certificate, so that I could obtain an extension of my leave, of which the following is a copy:

> Leave of Absence is hereby granted to Ensign Bakewell of the 3rd Battalion 27th Regiment of Foot, from the 12 November 1811 to 10 January 1812 in consequence of ill health;
> Given at the Horse Guards this 14 day of November 1811 by command of His Royal Highness the Commander in Chief.
>
> Castle Donington   W. Wynyard
> Leicester   D.A.G.

The contusion my chest had received at Abrantes now bore a dangerous aspect, having swollen prodigiously, and it afterwards broke and discharged a great quantity of matter, leaving two holes in my right breast and a smaller one in the

---

1   He is later referred to as Mr John Ridge, 44 Charing Cross, who was also regimental agent for the 8th, 47th and 67th, among other units.

centre of my stomach. The operation of having them probed hurt acutely: the pain almost unbearable. I was recommended to drink Port wine, lest the quantity of matter voided would cause a relapse.

I quit London on 6 November 1811 and took my place in the coach at *The White Horse*, Fetter Lane, for Castle Donington, which I reached at about noon next day, and found all my relations apparently well: I don't say friends, for that is a definition that is not always applicable to a relative.

Shortly after my arrival I applied to Dr James Farmer, a gentleman who had married a sister of my mother's, for medical advice. However, the little confidence I had in him soon dissipated, for he wished to make a hole in the bottom of my belly and open a drain between that and the others; but I would not let him try the experiment, thinking that he might not be able to close it again, as my flesh was quite black on the parts effected. I afterwards applied to Dr Eddewes of Loughborough. He was even more anxious to apply the knife than Dr Farmer, and proposed to cut me open all the way down that side and clean it out with a sponge. I didn't like the sound of that experiment either, so I went to Nottingham, where I found a district surgeon named White. He examined me, and recommended a certain diet which he thought would cure me without submitting to the danger of a knife; and this, in the event, together with bathing, did bring about a cure, but after quite a time.

Whenever the date of my leave of absence was approaching, Dr White used to supply me with a certificate, which was forwarded to the Adjutant General, who in response up-dated it to 24 September 1812, sending me a letter of confirmation of which the following is a copy:

Leave of absence is hereby granted to Ensign Bakewell of the 3rd Battalion 27th Regiment of Foot, from 25 August 1812 to

24 September 1812, but he must again appear before a military medical officer in order that a special report may be made on his case.

Given at the Horse Guards this 28 day of August 1812

by command of His Royal Highness the Commander in Chief.

Henry Calvert

A.G.

I thus prepared to visit London, and was just about to depart when I received the following from my Lord Moira, together with a copy of that in reply to one he had sent to the Horse Guards:

> Horse Guards
> September 1812
>
> My Lord,
>
> I have the honour to acknowledge the receipt of your Lordship's letter of the 10th instant, and state in reply that in consideration of the circumstances therein stated, the special medical report on the state of health of Ensign Bakewell of the 27th Regiment will be dispensed with.

General	I have the honour to be my Lord
The Earl of Moira K.G.	Your Lordship's most obedient
&c, &c, &c	Humble Servant,
Donington	Henry Calvert
	A.G.

As I had no knowledge of my Lord's intention of applying to the Horse Guards, the receipt of the above letter took me a little by surprise; and as I had intended to visit London anyhow, I did not let this prevent me, nor did I need to change the date on which I had planned to call on Dr Weir again. He examined me, and gave his opinion in a certificate to the Adjutant General stating that in his view I might be useful at the Depot, but he could not recommend me for actual service. The upshot of this intervention on my part was that I was ordered off to Scotland, which eventually was the cause of me tendering my resignation, with the following letter sent to the Earl of Moira in London:

> Loughborough
> 2 November, 1812

My Lord,

When I was last in town, I left a certificate obtained from the board at the Adjutant General's office, since when I have received their instructions to join at Ireland or North Britain. I should be obliged if your Lordship would inform me whether it is Newry or Ayr I am to proceed to.

To the Rt. Honble	I have the honour
The Earl of Moira,[2]	My Lord
London	Your most obedient Servant
	R.B.

And in reply:

Sir,   London, 4 November, 1812

The depot is fixed at Ayr in Scotland, and Lieut Colonel Neynoe[3] is already settled there, with all the recruits: of course that is your destination.

To Lieut Bakewell	I have the honour &c &c
27th Regiment	Moira
Donington	

---

2   Bakewell adds the following note: 'On calling on Lord Moira, he asked me to go with him and dine with the Prince Regent, but I declined that honour: how thoughtless I was, for I have never since had the opportunity.

3   Formerly Major William Neynoe: see note on p.xxvi.

As soon as I had received this, I made preparations for my departure, but as I found I was a little short of cash, I applied to my father for a loan of £10, thinking that he would cheerfully speed me on this long journey, as I was far from being well (still three large ulcers on my breast), and having not troubled him for any money during my illness. I little doubted that he would help, but he refused. When I held my ensigncy, he would assist me occasionally, but on obtaining my lieutenancy he declared he would not give me sixpence. As soldiers seldom accumulate much money, I had little alternative but to call on Lord Moira, at that time in the country,[4] where I saw him and tendered my resignation; which he then refused to accept, stating that if I wrote to him when back in London he would either accept it or give a reason why not. I now recognised that I had made a gaff, for not only had my Lord obtained a prolongation of my leave of absence on full pay, with which I might have saved up the necessary amount for my expenses, &c. without troubling anyone; but I had, as a young soldier, been precipitate in insisting on another examination without an iota of need.

*

Bakewell now posted a memorandum to Lord Moira, as Colonel of the regiment, together with a covering letter, in which he apologised should there be any irregularity in sending it to him directly, rather than through the usual channel, and thanking him for the trouble he had already taken.

*

---

4   This would have been Donington Hall, a short walk west of Castle Donington.

Castle Donington, 2 December, 1812

Memorial from Lieut Robert Bakewell, 27th Regt.

This is to certify and explain the cause of his return from the Peninsula and the reason of his continued absence from the Regiment. It was the laborious and a fatiguing service in the campaign of 1811 that his illness may be attributed; and having appeared before a medical board in that September, on examination, they recommended me to return to England for the reestablishment of my health. The disorder subsided or increased under different circumstances and the professional men in vending their different medicines; and the results of their ministrations have not been as favourable as I had been led to expect. The particulars of my complaint were detailed in the certificate I obtained from Dr Weir on my examination in last October and left at the Adjutant General's office, wherein he recommended that I appear at the depot at or before the 10th ultimo; but a relapse was the cause of me not attending; and I suppose the illness which made me unable to obey was the reason for our Lieutenant Colonel returning me as absent without leave.

The statement outlined above will I trust justify my request to your Lordship to accept my resignation, and to give me leave to sell the commission I purchased, as I am fearful that a return to duty in the military service would occasion a repetition of the same inconveniencies.

*

In reply, Lord Moira wrote (dated 25 December: sic), accepting Bakewell's resignation, which was followed by another letter, dated 20 January, 1813, in which he stated:

*

It is a satisfaction for me to observe that I have obtained the commander in chief's permission for you selling your Lieutenancy, and not merely the Ensigncy which you had purchased. Mr Ridge has instructions to arrange the matter with the eldest ensign in the Regiment disposed to buy this step.

I remain Sir,

Lieut Bakewell   Your obedient Servant

27th Regt.   Moira

*

Bakewell goes on to sum up his situation:

*

It will be seen from this correspondence that I had quite retired from the military service, which decision was entirely my own, but I began to think that it would have been more politic for me to have solicited for retirement on half pay, as in that case, should I recover my health, I might have the opportunity of rejoining; but it was now too late. If I had done so, and at a later date made my exit, which from appearances was very probable, then my purchase money would have been given away and the £400 lost. I thus applied to Mr John Ridge, 44 Charing Cross, to know the value of these commissions; and he replied that the Lieutenancy commission might soon be sold, but as for the Ensigncy, one could not expect that selling for a considerable time, as three others which had precedence over mine were on sale in the same regiment. One Ensign Ruddock[5] of the 27th bought my Lieutenancy, for which the agent transmitted £150 of it to me, which made me flush of cash, and I began to think of the best way I could apply it for the benefit and recovery of

---

5   Ensign Robert Stewart Ruddach.

my health. I was strongly recommended to take the waters, and baths, and in the following July I went to Matlock and thence to Buxton, where I bathed most days, and I alternated at these places until September.

It happened that one day I sat at dinner next to a former naval surgeon, to whom I related my case. He remarked that he might be of use to me and, in the event, was of infinite service, for he mixed up some powders and told me to stir it into the wine I drank after dinner. They gave me much relief; and those powders and the bathing in the different waters greatly accelerated – if they were not the only causes of – my recovery.

With my health being completely re-established, I began to employ my time in as useful a way as circumstances would allow in my neighbourhood, as my prospects in the military sphere were entirely thwarted.

One day, having to go to Birmingham, I passed through Leicester and Coventry on my way and called in on my old berth in Coventry's High Street. The excursion kept me from home for a week. On my return, I learned that a great majority of both householders and freeholders at Castle Donington were very keen to establish a market there, as the town, containing almost 3,000 inhabitants, was at least nine miles distant from any other that held a weekly market. It would be very convenient to re-establish one, for it had at one time been granted a charter by the Lord of the Manor, but so long had elapsed since this had been taken advantage of that few folk had any knowledge of such a privilege.

*

And it was to the uphill task of re-establishing a local market that occupied much of Bakewell's time and energy for a number of months ahead.

Bakewell had added to his manuscript the following list of officers in the 27th Regiment, as follows, slightly edited. By 'Escaped', I can only assume he meant escaped being wounded.

*

Rank and Name	Where employed	Remarks
Lieutenant Colonel:		
The Hon. Sir Lowry Cole	Commanding the 4th Division	Lost part of his breast at Albuera
Sir John McLean	Commanding 27th	Shot through the thigh at Badajoz
Major:		
William Howe Erskine		Dangerously wounded at Badajoz
John Birmingham		Killed at Badajoz
Peter Nicholson		Returned to England ill
Captain:		
John R. Ward		Severely wounded at Badajoz
John Smith		Killed at Badajoz
William Moore		Returned to England ill
Dawson Kelly	Staff appointment	Exchanged to the 27th
Archibald Mair	Staff at Belém	Escaped (since superseded)
Edward J. Elliott		Escaped (resigned)
John Pring		Shot in the groin at Badajoz
M. White	Staff appointment	Died
Thomas Jones		Killed at Badajoz

Lieutenant:

Phillip Gordon		Slightly wounded at Badajoz (since dead)[6]
William McLean	Acting Paymaster	Escaped
W.F. Fortescue		Returned to England ill
James Davidson	Acting Adjutant	Severely wounded at Badajoz (since killed)
Alexis Thompson		Severely wounded at Badajoz (since killed)[7]
Thomas Craddock		Escaped (since shot through the nose)
Samuel Mangin		Escaped
George Lennon		Promoted in the Portuguese service
Thomas Furnas		Escaped
William Dobbin		Wounded at Badajoz (Promoted in the Portuguese service)
Thomas Radcliffe		Wounded at Badajoz (since killed)[8]
Charles Levinge		Killed at Badajoz
Francis Simcoe		Killed at Badajoz
Charles Crawford		Killed in Pyrenees
Thomas Moore		Slightly wounded at Badajoz
Michael White		Killed at Badajoz
John Atkinson		Exchanged into the York Rangers

---

6   This was not until receiving his fourth wound, at Vitoria.
7   At Salamanca.
8   At Salamanca.

Ensign:

James McChord		Killed at Badajoz
James Graham		Escaped
Featherstone Hanby		Shot through the thigh at Badajoz
Carlisle Pollock		Slightly wounded at Badajoz[9]
Hugh Gough		Slightly wounded at Badajoz (since killed)[10]
William Weir		Slightly wounded at Badajoz
William Hare		Returned to Ireland ill[11]
Frederick Harding		Escaped (since killed)[12]
James Pike	Engineer Staff	Escaped
Joseph Hill		Escaped (since lost his leg)[13]
William Sampson		Returned to Ireland ill
Robert Jocelyn Phillips		Dangerously wounded at Badajoz
Lewis McLean		Escaped
J. Warrington		Killed at Badajoz
Paymaster Samuel Franklin		Deceased
Quartermaster Thomas Theobald		Escaped
Surgeon William John Clarke		Deceased (at Lisbon 13.8.1811)

---

9   And again at Sorauren.
10   At Toulouse.
11   Mentally disturbed. See Chapter 10.
12   At San Sebastian.
13   At Vitoria.

Asst. Surgeons:

William Brock   Deceased (at Lisbon
                                                                            5.10.1811)

Henry Franklin   Escaped
   (joined the 27th
   in Sept.1811)

Killed, 8; Dangerously wounded 9; Slightly wounded, 7;
Deceased, 5; Returned ill, 7;
Exchanged 4; Escaped 11: Total 51.
Six of the others have been since killed, exclusive of the
wounded.

As for myself, I was first engaged at the Lines of Torres Vedras,
assisting to throw up the defences to protect Lisbon. I was at the
driving of the French from Santarém and at the engagements of
Pombal and Redinha, where we were successful, and was at the
retaking of Campo Maior, at the surrender of Olivenza, and
likewise at the siege of Badajoz; while at the battle of Albuera
I was stationed at Elvas, superintending the necessary supplies
of nearly 300 of the 27th Regiment wounded from Badajoz.
My colonel, Sir John Mclean, was among the number; and
General Cole arrived wounded from Albuera; and so I was not
immediately in the engagement, but with a few friends, we
selected an elevated situation where we saw the battle fought
and won. This was my first campaign.

*

*Bakewell's manuscript proceeds to give a summary account — often
inaccurate — of events which occurred between his return to England
and his decision to re-join the 27th Regiment, which he did on 17
January 1815. Apart from a fleeting reference to the final battle of the
war at Toulouse, I have found no mention made to even the major battles*

in which that regiment was engaged. Fortunately, we now have 'The Peninsular War Journals of Lieutenant Charles Crowe, 1812–1814', impeccably edited by Gareth Glover under the title An Eloquent Soldier.[14] But Crowe did not disembark at Lisbon until late November 1812; thus it contains no description of the Salamanca campaign in the summer of that year. What is curious is that Bakewell makes no reference to that, nor to the Vitoria campaign of the following year, or to the several battles which were to take place in the Pyrenees (notably Sorauren), the siege of San Sebastian, and the battles of the Nivelle, the Nive, and Orthez, among others.

It is now virtually impossible to say to what extent news of them may have filtered back to Castle Donington after the events concerned. Bakewell does not admit to them having impinged on him in any way, or at least he took it for granted that the war might continue indefinitely, which, until the Capitulation of Paris at the end of March 1814, it did.

---

14   First published in its entirety in 2011 by Frontline Books.

II

In France, 1815

CHAPTER 15

Again on the Strength

It is difficult to know precisely what motivated Robert Bakewell — his health entirely re-establish by then — to rejoin the 27th Regiment. However, after a certain amount of correspondence, he was successful in his application; his rank as Ensign was confirmed; and in early February 1815 he received instructions to report to the officer commanding at their Depot on the Isle of Wight on or before 9 March. Bakewell's narrative continues:

*

HAVING AGAIN GOT PLACED ON the establishment, my duty was to make my preparations for departure. As I had £40 due to me as interest on my purchase money, which had been lying dormant for two years, this sum enabled me to join the regiment whether or not I received any assistance from my friends; but unexpectedly my father unstrung his purse and gave me £50. I thought it strange, but there is no accounting for some people's behaviour; for when I was unwell and ordered to join the 27th in Scotland, and without funds for the long journey, my father would not give me even £5.

Naturally, I accepted the gift, and on 15 March I set out from Castle Donington, riding to Loughborough, and there boarded the 'Briton' Coach, which traversed Leicester, Market Harborough, Northampton, Newport, Woburn, Dunstable, and St Albans to reach London next day. I stayed at *The Angel*, Angel Street, St Martin's Le Grand until the 19th, during which time I brought the necessary trappings needed. There is a house in St Martin's Lane, Charing Cross, which stocks a great assortment of military equipment and at far more reasonable terms than any other place I know of. Here I acquired an elegant sabre, as good as new, for 40/-, which would have cost 84/- elsewhere. I supplied myself likewise with military belts, a brace of pistols, and several other essential articles, equally cheap. Numerous officers resort to that particular establishment, both to buy and sell.

On my way there down the Strand on the 18th, my attention was drawn to a huge notice in one of the printers' windows stating that Bonaparte had escaped from Elba, and going on to give an account of his landing in France and progress to Grenoble, further details of which would appear in the evening paper.

Now, thinks I to myself, I haven't joined the 27th Regiment a second time for nothing; so later on I went to No. 7 Cheapside and bought a valise for 4 guineas; and next day I took my place on the 'Britannia' Coach for Petersfield, where I slept. I reached Portsmouth at about noon, only to find that the regiment had moved from their barracks on the Isle of Wight[1] to those at Hilsea. I repaired to the latter immediately; called on Sir John McLean, and gave him the letter from the Adjutant General. Having read it, he threw it into the fire, and ordered me to double up with Lieutenant Johnson. (Doubling is the term applied when two officers sleep in the same room, if there were no others vacant.)

Hilsea Barracks are good quarters in a pleasant neighbour-hood, but I did not stay long there, for on the 23rd the regiment was ordered to move to the new barracks at adjacent Gosport,

---

1   At Newport.

and as agreeably situated.[2] Here, I paid Mr Mackay, our Paymaster, the necessary fees for my new commission.

*

The internal organisation of the barracks and the miscellaneous duties of the commissioned and non-commissioned officers are described by Bakewell in inordinate detail before he returns to a subject that would seem to have rankled. Having heard that there was a Lieutenancy of the 27th Regiment to be disposed of, for which he was in line, Bakewell applied to his father, but as 'my old Daddy would not come down with the pence' (as he described it), he was unable to re-establish himself in the rank held prior to his resignation.

On 8 May, seven companies of the 1st Battalion of the 27th Regiment disembarked at Portsmouth from America, and 'a sumptuous dinner was provided for these gentry.'

*

Great mirth was excited by the stories of these military adventurers, and wine flowed freely; so much so that I was intoxicated with liquor for the first time since I entered the service. I did manage to walk out of the Mess Room unperceived, and immediately on reaching the lawn in front of the Barracks, I lay down. Captain Butler found me,[3] and saw me lodged safely in the Guard House, where they made me a temporary bed on the floor, and there I slept until the following morning, to awake not knowing where I was; but the officer on the Barrack Guard for that evening had been more unfortunate than I. While at the Mess table, both Carroll and his chair fell

---

2   Hilsea was a northern suburb of Portsmouth; Gosport lies to the west of Portsmouth Harbour.

3   This may have been Captain William Butler, who had been wounded in the Pyrenees.

backwards,[4] and he could only recover himself with difficulty; and we were not the only two.

On 13 May, together with Ensign Samuel Ireland,[5] I went again to Newport, where I paid Davies 11 guineas for a Regimental jacket including the epaulet. We returned to Gosport next day to find that, meanwhile, orders had been received for us to prepare, in as complete a manner as we were able, the seven companies of the 1st Battalion present, for it was intended that they should embark for the Continent with as much dispatch as possible. The remaining three companies, which were expected to arrive from America in the Headquarter Ship, were to follow them as soon as re-equipped.[6] On the 15th, these seven companies were paraded on one side of the Barrack Yard, and the 2nd Battalion on the other; and, from the whole, 700 of the most active and able rank and file were chosen to embark on the following day at Portsmouth for Ostend.[7]

My comrade Handcock had gone to see his brother, who was already aboard the transport with this detachment, and had been persuaded by him to accompany them.[8] The Commanding Officer would have had no knowledge of this decision, but officers volunteering their services in similar circumstances had little cause to expect disapproval.

On 5 June a Ball was held in Portsmouth in honour of His Majesty's Birthday (the 4th being a Sunday), when Lieutenant Johnson and I went to *The Crown Inn*, where we found a

---

4   Probably Ensign William Carroll.

5   Ensign Samuel Ireland was killed at Waterloo.

6   They had arrived on 5 June.

7   The latter part of Chapter 16 and Chapter 17 of *An Eloquent Soldier* (see Bibliography) provide Lieutenant Charles Crowe's contemporary description of events, when he was acting as Adjutant to Neynoe, and of his clash with him.

8   Both of them were to be wounded at Waterloo.

crowded assemblage, by far the most magnificent one that I had yet seen. Some of the Admirals and Naval Captains were literally covered with stripes and gold lace. We obtained two very pleasant partners with whom we danced until nearly 4 o'clock, by which time the greater part of the company had retired. Another grand dinner was held two days later for the second lot of officers to celebrate their arrival from America.

On the following morning I met Colonel Neynoe, who accosted me, commenting that I had a damned handsome sabre, and would I be prepared to sell it. I said I would not, but if he had a mind to accept it, I would make him a present of it, which I did; and he retained it throughout his time in France.

These were gay quarters for us. Dr Maxwell and I had three rooms between us – that is two bedrooms and a sitting one for our breakfast and suppers, which we used to club for – for we dined at the Mess, except when our fair friends used to visit us, which was twice each week. They used to mend our linen and keep our stockings and handkerchiefs in repair; but we could never learn who they were, for they would never let us see them at home nor tell us their names. They had introduced themselves to us one day by sending me a note when we were promenading, but on the first occasion we went out with them it was with difficulty that we could prevail on them to enter the Barracks, where indeed a great degree of immorality took place. They were elegantly dressed in silks, and the only expense to us was in feeding them.

Orders were received on 10 June for the three companies which had recently landed to follow as rapidly as possible the seven which had previously embarked. Colonel Neynoe had asked me whether I entertained any wish for half-pay; if so, he would get me placed on that establishment, but I replied that, due to the war unexpectedly recommencing, I would rather accompany him to the Netherlands. Although he was very tall

– well over six feet – and no less than 18 stone in weight, I thought I would have as good a chance as he in the field. He answered that if that was what I really wanted, he would arrange the exchange, as it was the 3rd, not the 1st Battalion, to which I belonged. I then called on the Paymaster, who gave me a month's pay in advance together with the embarkation allowance, which funds enabled me to provide myself with anything else I needed. Here was an instance which convinced me how politic it was for subalterns to be on friendly terms with the officer commanding a battalion.

Our transport set sail from Portsmouth on the morning of 14 June. We had a fine breeze, and reached the Downs that evening, casting anchor about one mile from Deal, as we had to wait for a fresh convoy. This set sail for Ostend on the evening of the 16th, the 14-gun brig HMS *Sharpshooter* and HMS *Snap* (12 guns) protecting seventeen other transports. These contained the 1st Battalion of the 7th Fusiliers and a number of cavalry horses, but we could not make much progress, the wind being contrary, and reached no further than Ramsgate. But at 5.0 the next morning the wind suddenly changed and we hoisted our sails and set off at about 8 knots an hour. This brought us within three miles of Ostend that evening, where we remained overnight, the tide being against us. On Sunday the 18th it was very stormy and boisterous, the wind being so violent that the boats sent to convey us ashore thought it not safe to approach, least an accident occurred; nor could we proceed further, as our transport drew so much water.

As it was calmer next day, the boats were alongside us by 4.0 and ferried the detachment to the shore at Ostend, where we took a snack before boarding other vessels which were to take us by canal to Bruges. (The men complained of their rations on this voyage as they had done previously, not on the quality but the quantity, the cause being that the sailors had as much in the way of spirits and provisions distributed to them in two days as the soldiers had in three.)

The 27th Regiment had a pleasant passage to Bruges, arriving there at about 3 o'clock, where we found great rejoicing, for they had just heard of the great victory that my Lord Wellington had won at Waterloo on the preceding day.[9] While the officers were taking some refreshment, I went into an adjoining room and wrote a letter to England to give whatever particulars I could collect about this glorious event.

We did not stay long at Bruges, but proceeded to Ghent, reached at 4.0 next morning, where we halted, awaiting instructions as to what route to follow next day, when 1,000 French prisoners taken at Waterloo passed through under escort to the coast.

I had obtained a billet at Ledeberg, a small village adjacent to Ghent. My landlord was a distiller, and he retailed the best Hollands Gin at 10d a quart, and very good it was. On Thursday the 22nd we moved into the town, where I had been provided with a fresh billet at 82 Bruges Street. I noticed that, in these hot countries, the females were very kind to us, even those in our billets were universally so, thus there was no reason for us to stray in search of wandering sheep during our stay there.

Our Colonel, who has the reputation as being partial to the system of flogging, had several of our men brought to the drum head for irregularities which had taken place. A Court Martial was held, after which – being found guilty of the charges

---

9   Almost 700 of the 1/27th had been present at the battle, sustaining 478 casualties: 105 killed and 373 wounded. The regiment had formed part of the 10th British brigade, commanded by Major-General Sir John Lambert, itself part of Lieutenant General the Hon. Sir Lowry Cole's 6th Division. The latter was in England at the time, where on 15 June he married Frances, daughter of James Harris, 1st Earl of Malmesbury, and thus missed Waterloo.

brought against them – the Colonel had them flogged on the public promenade, where the peasantry stood staring with amazement, unable to believe that the culprits could so tamely submit to being punished so severely.

Major Brown, the commandant here, ordered us to proceed to Mons by the shortest road, which ran through Grammont,[10] not Brussels and the battlefield of Waterloo, and by taking this route we saved half a dozen miles. We left Grammont at 4.0 on the morning of the 25th, with the intention of reaching Mons that evening, but our road was so crowded with troops that we halted at Ghlin, a village a short league from it. This had been a long march for the men, at least nine leagues [c. 27 miles]. During the last two days, we met with great number of French prisoners taken at Waterloo and now on their way to England.

---

10   Now named Geraardsbergen, south-east of Ghent, and south-west of Brussels.

CHAPTER 16

The Advance on Paris

IT WOULD APPEAR THAT BONAPARTE'S intention had been to fight the Allied armies separately, and the longer he delayed the encounter the less chance he had, for the British were receiving reinforcements arriving from America daily, and the forces of the Northern Powers were also in motion against him. This was the supposed reason why Bonaparte attacked the Prussian Lines as early as 16 June, where a most sanguinary battle was fought [at Ligny].

However, despite being so mauled there, at Waterloo the Prussians were well prepared to act on the offensive, and they pursued the fugitive Frenchmen with all the ferocity and inhumanity of a set of barbarians. They dispersed and scattered them to such an extent that they were unable to regroup in sufficient numbers to oppose our progress towards the capital.

To hear the peasantry tell us of the terror, dismay, and confusion into which their soldiers had been thrown, was most interesting, for they said that the Cavalry, flying in all directions, would dismount, enter any dwelling they happened to pass, pull off their uniforms, and compel any occupant who had any to supply mufti; those who had none were forced to strip and exchange clothes. They would hide in cellars, bedrooms, and any refuge they could find: woods and plantations were teeming with disbanded infantry.

On this account, when traversing various towns on our march to Paris, we had to keep on our guard; for it was impossible to be certain whether any members of the families on whom we were billeted had been in the engagement or not. Pistols are useful companions in such circumstances, and were frequently used.

But to continue with an outline of our movements: on the 26th and 27th, Lieutenant Furnas and I marched the league from Ghlin into Mons, a town of some opulence and population in the French Netherlands,[1] where we met several officers of the 27th at an inn. After being hospitably entertained there, at 4.0 next morning, having received a fresh route, we set off towards Bavay, with Colonel Warren in command of the detachment.

Shortly before reaching it, we passed two large stones marking the frontier; and the moment we entered France we heard the sound of gunfire to the east. On ascending a hill, we could plainly see the Prussians storming Maubeuge; and also to our right, Valenciennes, which they were besieging, both these fortified towns being only a few miles from us. Had not the Prussians got there already, these may have well delayed our advance, both being well garrisoned.

Bavay was so gorged with troops that we were obliged to continue a league further to a small village where we were agreeably accommodated overnight. At 5.0 next day we proceeded to Le Cateau (-Cambrésis), likewise crowded out,[2] indeed so full that we marched on for a league to find billets in another village. In these, we were quite as comfortable as in larger places, our quarters being generally with farmers, who provided a plentiful table for us: the main dish was invariably a couple of their fowl, and the wine was excellent. The farmers here keep a great deal of poultry; their outhouses are numerous and the yards clean. The houses are stone-built and substantial, frequently very long, but only two storeys' high.

---

1   It had a population of c. 20,000 at that time.
2   It was briefly Wellington's Headquarters during his advance on Paris.

A form of proclamation had been printed on Louis XVIII's orders, in which his subjects were urged to supply our passing troops with good lodgings and three meals a day, and stated that they would be reimbursed at the earliest opportunity. However, the locals hadn't much confidence in such promises, nor did they expect him to succeed to the throne a second time. However, this made no difference to us, as we could always obtain enough food and drink, while the fair French misses would provide us with a tub-full of water as soon as we had settled in our billets after what they assumed had been a long slog. They were most considerate, insisting in taking off our stockings, washing our feet and drying them with a clean towel, which solicitude we could hardly have expected from pretty lasses in an enemy country, and could only conclude that it was the custom with their own troops, as we experienced it daily while on our march.

We quit Le Cateau early on the 3th for Le Catelet,[3] arriving there at 11.0 and dispersed to our billets; but we had hardly been there an hour when a throng of French troops – at least 3,000 of them – came parading through the streets, hoisting white flags and shouting '*Vive le Roi*'. They had previously formed part of the National Guard, but had laid down their arms and, having promised not to take them up again for the same cause, had been given permission to return quietly to their respective homes. Here I bought a little French pony to carry my baggage, for which I gave 31 dollars.

Early next day we marched from Le Catelet to Péronne, but found both the town and neighbourhood full of Belgian troops, and the King of France was also there, *en route* for Paris. It is a populous and handsome place, but as no quarters could be procured, we pressed on to the hamlet of Huish.[4]

---

3   It lies some eleven miles north of St Quentin.
4   No hamlet of this name has survived.

A French nobleman resided here in a very magnificent château, to which he invited several officers of our detachment to dine and billet. I was told there was room for me if I wished, but as I was one of the junior officers and with no change of clothes at hand, I excused myself; but about half of them accepted and were hospitably entertained. Yet some were disappointed, for although a plentiful dinner was placed before them, during which wine flowed; but not much was drunk, for the guests were expecting more later, as would have been the case in their own country; but here it was all swept away with the cloth, and no more was offered, although coffee was served.

After that, they strolled in the gardens and plantations before the main front, where a party of the peasantry had collected, and which, on their appearance, began to perform country dances. These were very different to the English, being attended by more frivolity and wantonness, and displaying far more sensuality than possessed by our own youths, as evident also in their penchant for flirtation and intrigue. I first saw waltz dancing here, a way of amusing themselves marked by a degree of lewdness and immorality.

Next morning we set off for Roye, seven leagues distance, and also very full, so we veered west to obtain billets in a village where I was well entertained, having plenty of a rather superior wine. On the following day, after another seven-league march, we reached Gournay [-sur-Aronde][5] at 2.0. We had noticed a great deal of damage and desolation on the way, caused by the Prussians, and reminding me of old times – as if I was again in Portugal – with hides of slaughtered cattle lying scattered on the roadside. Houses had been ransacked and plundered, and any furniture not removed had been burned. Doors, shutters

---

5   Not far north-east of Compiègne.

and even window-frames had been knocked out for fuel; and the places left deserted.[6]

At Gournay there were two or three of what we called Military Canteens, retailing wine and spirits, supplies of which we paid for, although so far on our march we had obtained provisions and beverages from our humble hosts without any expense whatever. At about 3.0 that morning the king passed through the town with a train of lamp-lit carriages and attendants carrying torches, making quite a blaze, and this flaming mode of travelling caused a rumour to spread that Paris had surrendered.

We quit Gournay before dawn for Pont Ste Maxence (on the Oise) and traversed several villages displaying the same desolation as the previous day: shells of houses and destroyed furniture; but the Prussians had been more moderate with the French than the latter had been with the Portuguese, and had usually burned only the contents, not the buildings, for no doors, tables or chairs could be seen; thus the French were receiving only a share of the destruction they had visited on other nations.

We reached Louvres next day,[7] after passing a number of Prussian military butchers slaughtering plundered cattle on the

---

6   One of several confirmatory descriptions is found in James Stanhope's 'Letters' (see Bibliography), in which, when writing on his approach to Paris, he states: 'This far have we gone without difficulty & in the utmost order, but since we have entered the Prussian line of march our comforts were materially diminished, havoc having wasted everything in the most wanton manner & the only answer given to remonstrance is that the French did the same in Prussia. I never saw their army in Spain commit ravages more systematically than these fellows. I am now in a beautiful chateau, all the furniture of which is broken, fine glasses smashed, books torn to rags, linens & curtain cut up to adorn the Prussian amazons. The wine vats broke & the wine wasted, all the poultry killed & left in the fields and in short every village is the same.'

7   Louvres lies just north-west of the Charles de Gaulle airport.

turnpike road, and a great scrambling there was among their troops for the beef. The stories we heard from the surviving peasantry almost made one shudder; and the only redress they could obtain were threats of retaliation and revenge. On arrival, we found Louvres almost deserted; however, Louis and his entourage arrived about half an hour after us, when he alighted to have breakfast, after which a priest performed Mass, the service of the Roman Church being celebrated daily before the king.

This same priest later approached me in the street, took hold of my arm and insisted that I enter his house, where he began to complain about some English troops quartered there: that they had broken the locks of his chest of drawer and boxes and made off with their contents. I immediately made enquiries and found that the culprits were the servants of Mr Blundell, Paymaster to the Artillery, who had been billeted on him. So when Blundell turned up, I remonstrated; but the marauders, when questioned, answered that although billeted on him, they could not get the Reverend Prelate to supply them with enough food, and they had therefore taken such steps which would compel him: was this not excuse enough.

Blundell pressed me to stay and dine, which I happily did as there was nothing to be had in the town for love or money. He and I, together with the priest, fed well, the latter generously loading the table with food and drink. Blundell and I then walked some three or four miles into the countryside, surprised to find orchards on both sides the road heavy with apples, pears, and cherries, then just ripe, to which we helped ourselves.

On our return, on passing a gentleman's seat, we entered into conversation with a fellow at the gate, who told us that the owner and his family had departed, taking most of the furniture with him, but had left the château and a great stock of the choicest wines and spirits in his care. He offered to supply us with these in quantity for little or nothing, as he expected the whole cellar to be swept clean at any moment. We took away as much as we could carry and gave him a little cash, with which he appeared well satisfied, saying that some money was better than none at all.

We quit Louvres on the 6th, and after some two and a half leagues reached the fields of St Denis, where we found the 27th Regiment bivouacked, together with all the effective units of the Army that had survived the battle at Waterloo. Lieutenant Colonel Hare,[8] Lieutenants John Betty, William Kater,[9] and John Ditmas[10] were the only officers we found on duty, together with nearly 300 rank and file, but that figure kept increasing gradually – not only with the addition of our detachment – and was soon 700 strong, as groups of wounded, both from our Regiment and others, were turning up daily from Brussels. It was on this day that the Allies first entered Paris, from which the 27th had encamped one league distant; but our stay here was short, for next day we marched through the town of St Denis, and I never saw any place as crowded as it was. The king had passed through during the previous evening on his way to the Palace of the Tuileries, which apparently he had reached without incident.

---

8   Brevet Major John Hare (d. 1847) had commanded 2/27th in late 1813–early 1814, and the 1/27th at Waterloo. After the battle, being one of the very few unwounded officer in the battalion, he was made brevet Lieutenant Colonel; Lieutenant Colonel in 1825.

9   Ensign Kater was very likely on baggage duty that day. He is referred to frequently in Lieutenant Charles Crowe's *An Eloquent Soldier*; see Bibliography.

10   Ensign Ditmas would appear to have been wounded, but presumably not seriously.

CHAPTER 17

The Occupation of Paris

From here on, Bakewell devotes an excessive number of pages in his manuscript to inordinately elaborate descriptions of the numerous monuments, palaces, and sites he had visited during his month in Paris, which rarely add to the main purpose of this volume, which is to concentrate on Bakewell's military experiences; but they may be referred to when pertinent, together with other of his passing comments of particular interest.

*

ON 7 JULY WE ENCAMPED in the garden exactly in front of the Château de Neuilly, lately occupied by the Princess Borgese, Napoleon's sister,[1] in which our divisional general, Sir Lowry Cole, had now taken up residence. The Right Brigade of his or the 6th Division was commanded by General Sir John Lambert,[2] and the 4th, 40th, and 81st regiments[3] were brigaded with us.

The gardens, skirted by the Seine, were most attractive, with ample walks, embellished by a great variety of shrubs, and small plantations; but their appearance soon changed: the hothouse frames, shrubs, and plantations disappeared, the former

---

1   Pauline Bonaparte (1786–1825). The château, built in 1751, was destroyed in the revolution of 1848.
2   General Sir John Lambert (1772–1847); he had commanded the 6th Division at the end of the Peninsular War.
3   For 81st, Bakewell had written 82nd in error.

forming doors for our tents, and the latter came in handy for kindling and making the pot boil.[4]

It was my turn for duty this day with the Regimental Guard as soon as it had taken up its ground; but, on the 9th, William Kater and I traversed the adjacent village of Neuilly on our way into Paris, a very pleasant walk, it being through the Court end of the city, with carriages and fashionables constantly passing to and fro on the road, named the Avenue de Neuilly. This is dead straight, of great breadth and well paved; while between it and the footpath flourish three or four rows of trees.

Neuilly is about two and a half miles from the Palace of the Tuileries, and a Triumphal Arch, begun by Bonaparte, is being built on an eminence approximately half way between them. Although in an unfinished state, timber scaffolding near the summit gave us some idea of the elegance of the eventual structure.

We passed through the arch and down the Champs-Elysées, flanked on either side by some thirty or forty rows of trees between the turnpike and the buildings, amongst which our Light Troops were bivouacked, right up to the Palais de Tuileries. The Gardens of the Tuileries, which are extensive, contain a very beautiful fountain, and its promenades are embellished by a number of elegantly placed statues on pedestals.

From there, we made our way along the Rue St Honoré to the Place Vendôme, in the centre of which rises a column of large dimensions encased in bronze, the metal apparently cast

4 Coincidentally, it was also on 7 July that Private William Wheeler of the 51st penned his first letter from Paris, or rather from their encampment in the Bois de Boulogne, adjacent to the road into central Paris from Newillee [sic], as he spelt it. Unfortunately, within days, they were busy cutting down trees to build huts, to such an extent that they could then see the Seine to the rear of the camp.

from captured Austrian and Prussian cannon. Having climbed to the summit, which commanded a wide view over Paris, and descended, we fortified ourselves with biscuits and wine at the Palais Royal,[5] after which we returned to our regiment by a different route, with troops encamped in every field we passed.

I called on Carroll after parade and breakfast next day, and we went directly to the Tuileries, at the entrance of which was a concourse of carriages containing a few members of the French nobility and several British military types. It was apparently the first day since his re-establishment on which the king held an audience, but it was thinly attended.

*

Apparently, any British officer in uniform was let into the Tuileries unchallenged, and Bakewell and Carroll were able to approach quite close to the king, around whom were only a few of his family and a handful of courtiers, 'for the Parisians, and the major part of the French people would not come near him.' He is described as 'a little corpulent', and as he had gout, he moved very slowly, 'and waddles greatly when he walks.'

A visit to the adjoining Palais du Louvre was left to the following day, after which Bakewell entered the purlieus of the Palais Royal, the paved porticoes of which served as promenades, resorted to by crowds of every nationality, apart from the French. Numerous jewellers' shops,

---

5   By this date the name applied to an extensive range of buildings and galleries surrounding the original palace, formerly known as the 'Palais-Cardinal' (having been built in the 1630s for Richelieu). In 1697 this had been given by Louis XIV to his brother and his heirs, and soon acquired an equivocal reputation. In the 1780s, Philippe-Egalité had added the houses around the gardens as a speculation and, under pressure of debt, had let them out as shops and cafés, which became a rendezvous of malcontents prior to the Revolution, as the police were excluded from entry.

together with those of milliners, others selling fancy toys, and those of similar tradesmen, occupied the ground floors, as did several traiteurs, coffee-houses, and news-rooms. One of them was English, where copies of such papers as The Pilot, The Star, The Times, *and* The Morning Chronicle, *might be read for half a* franc. *Bakewell continues:*

*

The second storey consists principally of restaurants or what would be termed eating- or chop-houses in England, where dinners are economically provided at short notice. The third story is supposed to be occupied by *putains* – which in English means courtesans. The old mistress of the bevy has what might be termed a show-room, with two doors. These fair damsels are admitted singly, walk through, and make their exit; and by the end of this review the visitor may have made his choice. Being so near the dining-rooms, these are very convenient to those youths who resort there for that purpose, to which they are here greatly addicted. In the fourth storey are gambling rooms, while the attics are supposed to contain the refuse [or refugees] from all the rest.

*

Before returning to their encampment, Bakewell and his friend dined at the Hôtel Massinot *in the* Rue de Castiglione. *While there, the king passed by in his royal carriage, 'as much unnoticed . . . as if it had been one taken from the stand.'*

*

For dinner, they gave us soup, a fowl and lots of vegetables; a small beef steak, and a bottle of wine each, for which we paid 25 *francs* between us. This house was considered rather an expensive one, but it is well supported: a great number of officers were there, principally Prussians.

*

Two days later, Bakewell, this time accompanied by Lieutenants Furnace and Armstrong, briefly revisited the Tuileries. There were many more people in attendance that previously, and even shouts of 'Vive le Roi'. *Then to the Palais Royal again, where they sauntered for two or three hours, enchanted by* les femmes, *remarking:*

*

The French ladies cut a great figure here: gay dresses, fascinating manners: assignations and intriguing is much in vogue. I went into one of the milliner's shops, apparently as respectable as any one of those in the square, where I bought a few pairs of gloves. The owner, a pert young lady, had another in her company, whom I assumed was a customer and with whom I flirted, saying '*Vol a vous*' [*Voulez-vous*: Would you like to?]' to which she replied 'We [*sic*] Monsieur'. Says I: '*la cushie* [*se coucher*, to go to bed], Mademoiselle', and she repeated 'We Monsieur'. Then, with the mistress of the shop, she accompanied me into an adjoining street, where she lived when not otherwise engaged, and where we amused ourselves. This pursuit was frequently repeated, as I often found her in the same shop at about the same time of day; but on one occasion I had apparently not taken notice of her at the door, which was the reason why she did not want to meet me again. I was told she was of a respectable family living not far from Paris, but that this was a widely followed practiced in France.

Although less reserved, I found the society of the mistress of the shop just as blissful. On first putting the same question to her, she replied in a way I couldn't understand, and I answered '*no entendre*', to which she responded '*No Rouge*'. I thought this meant 'No Red'. Armstrong, who was passing by, explained that she didn't care to walk out with any gentleman wearing uniform; but if I came in plain clothes, she would have no objection. He was very surprised to find that a young and apparently respectable female, seeming to be flush, allowed herself to follow such a wanton custom.

We dined that day at a second-floor restaurant. They gave us soup, boiled mutton, fish, roast veal, lots of vegetables, and fruit for our desert, with a bottle of Port wine each, which cost us 3 *francs* 10 *sous* each: one might term it an economical meal.[6]

At 7.0 we set off back to the camp, traversing the Champs-Elysées, off which there seemed to be several Waltz Rooms,[7] into one of which we went, as it was still only dusk. They were built in the form of a rotunda, with a circular dance-floor in the centre, which was surrounded by a 3-foot rail; and anyone wanting to dance might enter this enclosure on paying a man at the entrance, the amount varying in different places depending on their amenities. At this one, a *franc* was demanded. Those who don't choose to foot it are provided with seats outside this fence, where they could enjoy themselves over their wine or whatever liquor they ordered. I obtained a good partner and waltzed for the first time in my life, there being an excellent band. There are spacious gardens attached containing a range of secluded arbours to which couples may retire. Numerous officers in mufti attended these places of amusement, which are open daily, including Sundays, and they are generally crowded. We stayed there until almost midnight, having danced several waltzes and drunk a few bottles of Port, for which they charged a *franc* each, after which, it being a fine night, we had an agreeable two-mile walk to our camp.

---

6   Bakewell noted that 1 sou was the equivalent to ½d; 1 *franc*, 10d; 1 *Louis*, 16/8; 1 Doubloon, £3, 8/-, but because the coins circulated were of such variety: viz. Flemish, Dutch, etc., the tradesmen used to keep a table at hand which defined the value of each.

7   These would be described in France as *guinguettes*.

On 10 July, I saw for the first time my Lord Castlereagh,[8] who was walking arm-in-arm with my Lord Wellington, and was told that the former had only just arrived from England. On the 15th, I steered again for Paris and, as usual, we made our first stop the Palais de Tuileries, followed by the Louvre in order to see the paintings. There was an aged damsel[9] at the door who sold guide-books at a *franc* each, which contained an explanation of every painting, its artist, etc, all being numbered. We entertained ourselves here for some hours; indeed, we could have remained for weeks had our curiosity tempted us to stay so long.[10]

Next day, being a Sunday, the Division attended a drumhead Divine Service near General Lambert's quarters. I remained in the camp the rest of the day, during which lots of French girls visited our tents, offering fruits of various kinds, which we could buy at a very reasonable price; others came to make assignations.

I went into town on the 18th and – for the first time – found difficulty in entering the Tuileries, due to the crowds gathered there to get a view of the king, so I decided to go sight-seeing instead, first to Les Invalides, which like the Hospital

---

8   Robert Stewart, Viscount Castlereagh (1769–1822), had been Foreign Secretary since 1812, and the senior British Plenipotentiary at the recent Congress of Vienna.

9   An 'aged damsel' is a typical example of Bakewell's stilted English, rather than 'old maid'.

10   Bakewell remarked that the galleries were open every day from 9.0 until 6.0; that among the crowds were many 'fashionables', but only a few English ones, not many having arrived in Paris by then. As he described it, 'Blücher threatened to revolutionize these rooms, and send the plundered property home again': but this had not yet taken place. However, by 6 August, when Bakewell again visited the Louvre, he found the Prussians 'very busy in the Painted Gallery taking down those pictures and packing them in cases.'

at Chelsea, was occupied by maimed and disabled soldiers. I next visited the Palais du Luxembourg, in the gardens of which Prussian troops were bivouacked.

Later, with my friends, I went to dine at No. 65 Palais Royal, but inadvertently we went up two pairs of stairs instead of one, and ran into an old *putain* and her flock of a dozen tarts, at the sight of which we as rapidly descended, preferring to sit down to a good meal. Afterwards, we sauntered back through the gardens of the Tuileries, where there was a great deal of dancing and shouting of '*Vive le Roi*', and we enjoyed ourselves looking on and drinking wine until 11.0 at night.

*

Bakewell was on Barrier Guard next day, when there was a rumour current that Bonaparte had been caught in a blanket and had surrendered himself, but little credit was attached to it.

CHAPTER 18

The Occupation of Paris, continued

On Tuesday 18 July 1815, Bakewell, with a detachment under Captain Charles Pepper, marched four miles to relieve the guard at the gates below the hill of Montmartre,[1] their duty being to examine closely all packages either entering the city or going out, in particular the panniers being carried in on horses. They would ask whoever led them what they contained and, should the answer be fruit, they would occasionally plunge their swords through to be sure that the truth was being told, least any person be concealed in them.

The party fed at **The Grand Turk**, a convenient inn at which they were each charged 7½ francs for their breakfast, dinner, wine and spirits, etc., and when they asked for some Brandy grog that evening, they would be measured out a full quart of very good quality, for which the charge was only 15d.

Next day, they climbed up the hill of Montmartre (the ascent to which commenced just outside the walls), its summit commanding a wide view of the surrounding countryside. It was Bakewell's opinion that if a besieging army ever got possession of this height they might easily destroy the whole of Paris.

Bakewell and his companions also found 'a great many Waltz Rooms on this side of the town,' and spent a couple of hours in one of them,

---

1   The hill or 'Butte Montmartre' rises some 340 ft above the level of the Seine. It overlooks the northern section of the wall encircling Paris, erected by the farmers-general in the 1780s, which was pierced by numerous gates and toll-houses (of which four, designed by Claude-Nicolas Ledoux survive), at which a tax, the infamous *octroi*, was levied formerly on all goods entering the city.

where he danced with 'a lark-heeled fair one', who gave him 'a good seasoning.' Being on duty, they were unable to continue dancing for any length of time, but occasionally, throughout the evening, they would steal away briefly to take part in the frolic.

As the detachment was relieved by a guard of the 4th Regiment at 5.0 next morning, they were able to return to camp in time for breakfast, and to hear that, three days earlier, Napoleon had unconditionally surrendered to Captain Maitland aboard HMS Bellerophon *at Rochefort.[2]*

On the 22nd, Bakewell set off to visit the Jardin des Plantes, the extensive botanical gardens in the south-west quarter of the city, which greatly impressed him, and its exploration occupied most of the day.[3]

Bakewell was on duty next day when orders were received for both infantry and cavalry regiments to be paraded at 7 o'clock the following morning on the Neuilly road, where they would be reviewed by all the crowned heads then in Paris. Bakewell, proudly carrying one of the regimental colours, but being unsure whether or not he should lower the colours when royalty passed, asked Colonel Warren,[4] who told him to do whatever those of other regiments were doing. In the event, Warren himself was ticked off by Wellington for not appropriately presenting his sword when the illustrious party rode by, during which, as the highway was so very dry, they threw up such a cloud of dust that the colour of their uniforms could hardly be distinguished;[5] but as Bakewell remarked,

---

2   Captain Sir Frederick Maitland (1777–1839) had accepted Napoleon's surrender on 15 July.

3   These had been founded in 1626 as a 'physic garden' for medicinal herbs, and opened to the public in 1650.

4   Lieutenant Colonel Lamuel Warren (1771–1833).

5   This is confirmed by Colonel Sir Augustus Frazer amongst others, who remarked: 'The dust was intolerable.' Frazer also states that, at the review, there 'were 65,000 men under arms, of whom about 10,000 were cavalry and 4,000 artillery.'

an inspection such as this had been was such a rare event that there were no precedents which could be followed.

On the 31st, on crossing the Pont d'Iéna (or 'de Jena'), which Blücher had threatened to demolish,[6] Bakewell chose to revisit Les Invalides, and then walked to the Palais Bourbon, which also greatly impressed him.

Next day, Bakewell sent his servant James Drum into Paris to buy provisions such as tea, sugar, butter, and spirits for both himself and Kater; but apparently Drum got drunk while on his way back; had misbehaved, and thus locked up overnight by the French authorities. Although released next morning, when his pony was returned to him, there was no sign of his purchases, nor had he any recollection of where he might have mislaid them, which occasioned the loss of 3 Napoléons,[7] for which dereliction of duty, although threatened with a good flogging, he was merely dismissed.

A day or so later, Bakewell noticed two or three peasants digging within a few yards of his tent, where they excavated not only a gold watch-chain and four gold seals, but also extracted three bags of gold said to have been secreted there by one of the princesses previously occupying the Château de Neuilly. Bakewell does not say whether or not they were permitted to make off with their treasure.

---

6   Frazer, writing on 12 July, states that the Prussians had started to destroy the bridge: 'They had removed masses of masonry from two of the beautiful arches in order to blow it up; but they have been stopped, and the bridge is now the Pont de l'École Militaire . . .' Wellington later remarked that Blücher had made the attempt, but 'the Prussians had no experience in blowing up bridges. We, who had blown up so many in Spain, could have done it in five minutes. The Prussians made a hole in one of the pillars, but their powder blew out instead of up, and I believe hurt some of their own people.'

7   A 'Napoléon' was the colloquial name for a gold coin worth 20 *francs* then in circulation, depicting the Emperor's features on the obverse.

On 3 August, with Furnas,[8] the Paymaster, together with a friend from the 29th Regiment, Bakewell made up a party and rode a short league to visit the Château de St Cloud,[9] with its beautiful cascade and fountain-embellished gardens. Bakewell was astonished by the extravagantly decorated interior: and it is of interest that — doubtless due to his former familiarity with fabrics — he described in detail the crimson velvet carpeting, and those of Napoleon's bed in particular: it was

stuffed with cotton wool; the blankets of a similar material to our Patent Fleecy Hosiery, and the sheets of fine damask woven into a variety of figures; the pillow-cases and covering quilts were of rich fine white satin; the curtains of fine India tambour muslin, with an amount of gold balls interspersed all over it, and bordered with a broad gold fringe. I borrowed a pair of scissors and cut one corner off one of the blankets and brought it away with me . . .

From there, they visited an extensive building just outside the gates, which contained a vast display of porcelain, much of it presumably from the former Sèvres factory, which although destroyed by fire some forty years earlier, had been revived and was now under State control. Bakewell and his party watched the various stages of its manufacture and decoration, in which a great number of people were busily employed with their paint-brushes.

On the following evening Bakewell and his friend Handcock attended the Opéra Comique,[10] at the entrance to which they were each charged

---

8   He may have been related to the three brothers Furnace [*sic*] listed in Hall's *Biographical Dictionary*.

9   Napoleon's second marriage, to Marie-Louise, had been celebrated there in 1810. The château was burnt out during the German occupation of 1870, but not demolished for another two decades.

10   It would appear that Handcock's wound at Waterloo was slight.

6 francs and 12 sous for admittance to the boxes, which were already packed; but probably because they were wearing uniform, a party of French installed in the box immediately vacated the front row of seats for them. With their limited knowledge of the language, they were unable to appreciate fully the entertainment offered, although some ladies in an adjacent box seemed highly diverted by it.

*

Handcock, in his best French (which was slight) addressed one of them with '*Val a vous spouse* [sic], *Mademoiselle*' [*Voulez-vous m'épouser?*: Will you marry me?], to which she promptly replied '*We Monsieur*'. He hardly expected such a complaisant response, the result of which was that at midnight, after the drama was over, he accompanied her home. Meanwhile, I entered a restaurant in the Palais Royal, where I waited; and after half an hour he joined me. We had some cold chicken and drank two bottles of what they called English Porter, for which they charged 2 *francs* each, and were back in camp by 2.0.

*

Next day, together with Furnas, Smith, and Carroll, Bakewell hired a coach and after calling in at the Tuileries, where they saw the king pass through the Hall of Marshals as was his usual habit at midday — when he complimented them with a salute — the party drove on past the Palais du Luxembourg. The excursion continued some half a mile beyond the city walls to what were called the Catacombs, the entrance to which appeared to be cut into the wall. Here they each paid a franc to an attendant before following the guide along an interminable series of passage, eventually entering 'the marrow of this secret and dismal prospect of a very large collection of human bones, piled in heaps about 4 foot wide and 7 foot high . . .' At last, and with some relief, they saw the light of day at the end of a tunnel, returned their torches to the guide, regained their coach, and drove back to camp and dinner.

On another occasion, together with Furnas, Bakewell rode some four miles south-west to the Château de Malmaison,[11] then occupied by Lord Combermere, commanding the British Cavalry,[12] passing one of his aides on approaching the place.[13] Despite being in uniform, on applying to enter the building, they met with a rebuff for the first time, being told that a ticket of admission was necessary: unfortunately, neither of them carried any cash.

On Sunday, 6 August, on going into town, Bakewell was surprised to find all the tradesmen's shops open and business of all kinds being transacted to the same extent as it would be on any other day of the week, and commented that should there be any alteration of the peoples' pursuits on the Sabbath, it was certainly not in favour of religion, or morality, but rather as a Field Day for sports and amusements. Bakewell described that evening, when he returned to camp.

*

Officers would frequently dine with each other, and Kater and I dined with Lieutenants Glynne and Atkinson of the 40th Regiment,[14] returning to our tent at about 11 o'clock. Just as I was about to fling myself down between my blankets on my bed of straw, I heard a female voice from outside murmur that

---

11   It was here, some distance west of Neuilly, that the Empress Joséphine had lived in retirement after her divorce from Napoleon on 1809, and where she had died five years later.

12   Sir Stapleton Cotton, Viscount Combermere (1772–1865), a Major General in 1805, he commanded the Cavalry in the Peninsula, and the Allied cavalry in the Waterloo campaign, and was later Commander-in-chief in Ireland, and India, and field-marshal in 1855.

13   This was the Hon. Augustus Stanhope (1794–1831), a son of the Earl of Harrington, whom Bakewell remembered as having been a cornet in the 12th Dragoons.

14   This was Lieutenant Andrew Eugene Glynne, who had been wounded two years earlier at Sorauren. His companion was Ensign George Atkinson.

she was lost. Naturally, I replied '*Entre Mademoiselle*'. But as soon as daylight appeared, I found she wanted no instruction about which way to go: but similar incidents occurred on most days.

Being the officer on Forage duty on 7 August, I had my party paraded by 5 o'clock, mounted my pony, and we set off from our encampment to some fields some two miles beyond the gates on the far side of Paris. While cutting our corn, which was almost ripe, our exertions were watched with great curiosity, but from a respectable distance, by a party gathered on a nearby hill. This is fairly open cultivated country, wheat being the staple crop, except when covered by several acres of oats and kidney-beans. We loaded our horses with enough for the whole regiment; but the owners of the property, although seeing us cut and carry it away, made no complaint, knowing that it was useless to do so. This foraging took place every day, and as the quantity required was very considerable, almost all the fields I could see were cleared. When my party was loaded up, I sent it back to camp in charge of a sergeant: being mounted, I wanted to take the opportunity of returning through town.

I entered by the Porte St Denis, and my first port of call was at a barber's, distinguished by its pole. On knocking at the door, a dashing, delicately-framed female appeared, who gave be a clean shave, which was the only time that one of her sex had shaved me. I then returned to camp.

Later that day, I rode back to the Champs-Elysées, entered one of the Waltz Rooms, and found a pretty partner, with whom I danced all evening, and walked off with her, not getting back to my tent until 1.0 in the morning. There were many French officers there in mufti; and I was told that no less than ten thousand were in Paris, thus dressed. *En route* to our bivouac, I was overtaken by two or three of them in search of an English soldier who had taken one of their new hats, leaving his old cap in its place, which caused them to swear not a little.

*

On 10 August Bakewell went to view the Duke of Wellington's residence, which was only two hundred yards distance from the gates of the Tuileries Gardens, while a few hundred yards further on, in the Rue du Faubourg St Honoré, was that of Lord Castlereagh's, which Bakewell also passed by before making his way to the Palais de l'Elysées, then occupied by the Emperor of Russia.

*

Soon after I had entered the courtyard, the Emperor made his appearance and took his guard by surprise; but they formed and presented in double quick time: it was almost instantaneous.

A little beyond it was the Hôtel of Prince Berthier,[15] on the boulevards, which was the Emperor of Austria's residence, while the King of Prussia had taken up his quarters some distance beyond.

*

At the end of his circuit, and soon after Bakewell had returned to his tent, a sergeant entered with the Orderly Book, in which he found that he was instructed to take command of a detachment of Limited Service men belonging to the 4th, 27th, and 29th regiments, and proceed with them to Ostend, a distance of no less than 200 miles. As it was already 7 o'clock, he had little time to make the necessary preparations, having to set off at 4.0 next morning.

*

I had to receive the mens' balances from the officers who commanded the company to which they belonged; to call on Lieutenant Colonel Wilson, who would furnish me with a route;

---

15   This was the former residence of Alexandre Berthier, Prince de Wagram (1753–1815), who had very recently died (on 1 June, at Bamberg in Bavaria).

and also to find conveyances for any baggage and any disabled men, who could not make the journey without such assistance. I found Colonel Wilson at his billet at about 8.0, together with his pretty young Miss. I explained my business, and he at once referred to his map, and drew my route. He included Brussels in the line of our march; but on me commenting that by going from Mons to Ghent via Ath would save five or six miles, being shorter than via Brussels, he made that alteration. I rather wished I had not noticed this, as the route originally drawn would have taken me through the field of Waterloo.

CHAPTER 19

The March to Ostend

AT 4 O'CLOCK ON 11 August, together with two sergeants, a corporal, and thirty-three men of the 27th Regiment, six of the 29th, one of the 4th, with the addition of two women and two children, I took my leave of our camp at Neuilly.

We set off through St Denis for Louvres. After about four miles, a fair-featured young lady overtook us, begging that I would let her accompany the detachment to England: she wished to return to her friends in Ireland, her husband having been killed at Waterloo. I consented for two reasons: one, to accommodate her; and secondly as a distraction for myself.

Next day, *en route* to Pont Ste Maxence, we met numbers of wounded from several regiments, among them the 88th, who had been recuperating at Brussels, and also those of three German regiments. On reaching Senlis, which was very crowded, I applied to the Commandant, a sturdy black-bearded Prussian, for a fresh conveyance, but he was most unaccommodating; not at all disposed to assist, his favours being reserved for his countrymen.

Pont Ste Maxence, being occupied by the 5th Division, was also congested, so we pressed on to the village of Beauparne, where I billeted myself on the Mayor, a farmer, who provided a couple of chicken for dinner, vegetables in plenty, and also good wine, but that I could always find in these villages. Although our men's rations were drawn daily, and signed for in the usual way, I had no idea what arrangements these private individuals may have in the way of being reimbursed by the French Government, for they never asked for our names or any confirmation of what we had eaten.

At 5.0 next morning we continued our march, first through Gournay-sur-Aronde, meeting a strong detachment of foreigners and also a troop of the 3rd Dragoon Guards commanded by Captain Edmund Storey, whose parents lived at Lockington.[1] The rest of the 3rd Dragoons, together with the 3rd Regiment (the Buffs) were there as well, so we were obliged through the lack of any accommodation to push on to Margny-sur-Matz, a short distance to the right.

We passed a brigade of Belgian artillery and some Prussian cavalry next day while on the road to Roye; but as this was also full, partly in the possession of the 4th Regiment of Foot,[2] we spent the night at adjacent Gruny. Our road now veered north-east, on which we crossed with the 3rd Battalion of the 27th. It was almost 6 o'clock by the time we reached Bellenglise (north of St Quentin), only to find it crammed with Prussians.

Here, I found a billet in the château, a handsome building,[3] in which some fifty men from one of the Prussian units had already installed themselves, and for whom a table with a fine damask cloth had been set for dinner. The owner was an elderly gentleman with a wife and two daughters. They were attended by several servants, who served the soldiers the moment the meal was ready, which consisted of soup, a variety of dishes, and wine in plenty. The Prussians treated them abusively, saying they would not be served by them, but by their masters,

---

1   This village lies immediately east of Castle Donington.

2   The King's Own had fought at Waterloo in Lambert's Brigade.

3   The gates only of the château survived the desperate fighting here in late September 1918: near its site rises an Australian war memorial.

to whom they behaved with gratuitous insolence, at which the two daughters sought my intervention. I went into the dining-hall, which the officer in command of the party was about to leave, and remonstrated with him, at the same time admitting that I had no right to interfere.

Meanwhile, having taken their fill, his men had left the table (each taking a full bottle under his arm), lurched into the garden, and started to help themselves to any fruit they could find in the orchard before stretching out below the trees. When it became dark, by then intoxicated, they re-entered the château, demanding spirits, which were immediately supplied in abundance. They proceeded to pour all the brandy they were unable to drink into several large bowls, took off their shoes and socks, and washed their feet in it before returning the bowls to the owner with insulting guffaws. The rabble then spread their coats and blankets on the floor of the dining-hall. Here they remained dormant until dawn when, soon after a breakfast of hot coffee and toast, they set off.

My own party had acted with great moderation, and our host and his family thus treated us with all consideration. I had not been long in my room before the cook had come to enquire what I would like for dinner. He had a 'frenchified' appearance – frizzled hair, frills, a white apron, and silk stockings. On asking for one substantial dish only – as it had been a long march, and I was tired – I was served with a fillet of roast veal, a piece of boiled beef, vegetables, and a plentiful dessert. Meanwhile, one of the daughters had brought me two bottles of champagne concealed under her apron.

After dinner, our host, who appeared to be strongly prejudiced in favour of Bonaparte, spent the rest of the evening with me. He thought it a hoax, and quite ridiculed the idea, when I told him that the Emperor had been made a prisoner and would be sent to St Helena, being convinced that it was a mere rumour intended to coax the French people to favour Louis's party.

Other Prussian units had been billeted among the villagers. Having consumed all they possibly could, apparently they had compelled their hosts to find more; and when, before leaving, they were asked to pay for at least what they had had in the first place, reacted by smashing the windows with the butts of their muskets. Seeing this going on, I demanded the reason for such violent behaviour, at which they retorted that this was how they chose to discharge French bills and enjoy the sweets of retaliation.

On the 16th we marched to Le Cateau (through which we had passed on our way to Paris), to meet the 6th or Inniskilling Dragoons and the 2nd or Queen's Dragoon Guards. Here I overtook Lieutenant Moffatt of the 71st Regiment on the same errand as myself, with a group of Limited Service men under his command. As instructed, we remained there all next day to rest. This was the cause of an outcry against my men, for as spirits were very cheap here, those on whom they were billeted had provided so much that they had become quite drunk, and some had repaid the kindness in a barbarous way: Thomas McCullogh and Daniel Hammell had stripped the females in their billet quite naked, grossly insulted and even threatened to murder them; so I put them in the Guard House at once. Others had created disturbances in several parts of the town, even fighting pitched battles, which caused the Town Major (Johnson of the 71st) to complain of their conduct; and it required great exertions on my part to subdue and discipline them.

Next morning, we set off towards Bavay, leaving the two prisoners behind, only to find them joining us soon after, liberated by the Commandant as being unwelcome and troublesome guests. After the 'field day' of Le Cateau, I gave orders that no more spirits should be supplied other than the amount regularly issued; but it was of little use, for the men would immediately leave their billets, chose other quarters, and get intoxicated at the expense of their new hosts. However, as Bavay was full of Prussians, we proceeded to the neighbouring village of Hon [-Hergies], where I was billeted with the Mayor and given a good dinner of eggs, frizzled bacon, lots of vegetables, and soup: wine was always available in quantity.

An English merchant who had followed us from Bavay, having some British-manufactured goods with him and being nervous that they would be seized either by French citizens or the Prussians, pressed me to allow some packets to be hidden at the bottom of our cart, offering me any remuneration I liked. I complied with reluctance, but refused any payment.

Next day we moved from Hon to Mons, passing the 81st Regiment and several strong detachments of British infantry on their way to Paris. Mons being as crowded as were most of the larger towns, we carried on to Jurbise, where I was quartered in the château. Here, I was given a very curious dinner, the first course being a tureen of boiled milk in which sugar and spices had been added, followed by a dish of artichokes; and after that, a very small veal cutlet without vegetables, the meal being concluded with butter and cheese. When serving meat and vegetables, they rarely place them together on the table, but one after the other; and, when the cloth is removed, nuts are provided, and plenty of wine. I could have preferred a more substantial meal, with beef steaks and a 'murphy', and drink; but the change was well-timed.

August 20th being a Sunday, we started early for Grammont,[4] with a wagon and horses in lieu of a cart, arriving there at 2 o'clock. I obtained a billet with a physician, who treated me with every kindness, provided a good dinner, and invited some

---

4   Now named Geraardsbergen.

intimates to join us that evening. They enquired about a Colonel Henry Ellis of the 23rd, the Welch Fusiliers, who had been billeted there for some time prior to the battle of Waterloo, and expressed genuine sorrow at hearing of his death in that engagement.[5]

I observed my host's daughter in conversation with Charles O'Neil (my new servant), who was well versed in their language. On enquiring what rank I held, he had answered 'A Captain, *Mademoiselle*', at which she asked him to let me know that she would much like to join me on the tour and would defray her own expenses. I was unlikely to reject such a proposal, the more so because it happened that my frolicsome partner from St Denis had fought shy and bolted by then, making room for any accidental casualty that might present herself. So she sent for her friends, took leave of them, and started to pack up her clothes ready to set off. However, the old boy, smelling a rat, had set a close watch on his daughter, and to prevent her escape had secured her bundle, so that when we marched off on the following morning for Ghent, *Mademoiselle* was left behind: but she promised to manage things better on my return.

We met the 57th on their way to Paris. (I forgot to mention that on the previous day we had also met the 9th, 16th, and 91st regiments, which had been in America previously, also on their march there.) The colonel of the 57th had a prisoner with him which he bid me to lodge in the Ghent Guard House. Named William Critchley, he was a private in the 6th Regiment, and by chance they had caught him deserting. On reaching Ghent, I placed him under guard, but was then informed that as the 6th was quartered only three miles away, the Provost would send him back to them under escort.

---

5   Lieutenant Colonel Sir Henry Walton Ellis (1782–1815), 23rd. He had died two days after the battle, from a wound which was his seventh.

Today, 21 August, I obtained a billet in a house belonging to a colonel who had commanded the 121st regiment under Bonaparte, of whom he was a strong partisan; indeed, the colonel had fought at Waterloo, there receiving a musket wound in his neck. He told me that when in Spain he had frequently been engaged with our regiment.[6] We remained there next day, where I again encountered Lieutenant Moffatt, who accompanied me to the Commandant, Major Brown of the 23rd, who immediately recognised me, for the old soldier had been Commandant at Elvas formerly. He asked to see my route, at which he gave me a fresh one, and ordered boats to be in readiness next morning to convey our detachments to Ostend via Bruges by barge – a far more convenient way than by land – and so we had no need to press wagons.

I suppose Ghent must contain 100,000 souls.[7] It was the only place in which I found it hard to know where I was, for the canal winds in various directions through the streets, and the bridges are all similar and in such numbers as to confuse the stranger. I could always find my way in London, Paris, Lisbon, Dublin, and any other large city I knew, but in Ghent, if I went a quarter of a mile from my billet, it was always a matter of doubt whether or not I would need a guide to get home. Moffatt and I spent the evening at the adjacent inn, where we used to dine when the 27th when previously there. Of all the towns through which we passed, it was perhaps the most accommodating: apt was the adage that a sailor may find a wife in every port, for our hostess in almost every house we lodged would be most amiable.

Early next morning the boats were ready to embark our men. Moffatt, like myself, found great difficulty in collecting

---

6   This is doubtful, for the 121e Ligne were largely engaged in or near the Levant coast. The colonel may have been Joseph Clément Renouvier.

7   In fact, the normal population at that time was a little over 60,000.

them together due to the fact that, having been at Waterloo and expecting their discharge daily, they felt privileged, and would make freer than usual with their intake of spirits; and as a glass of brandy or Hollands could be bought for a penny, it was hard to keep them sober.

However, by 9.0 we had them all aboard the barges. These were constructed like a Turnpike road, being high in the centre and sloping towards the sides, but without any railings to prevent lumber rolling overboard. No matter how attentive one might be, should anyone accidentally trip, there was a danger of being precipitated into the water. As most of our men were inebriated, on falling asleep, some would roll like logs down the side of these vessels and drop into the canal. By the time we had sailed three miles there was almost a score of them swimming behind us like so many spaniels: it was fortunate for them that they could all swim. Although the ducking had the effect of sobering them up, at least one of them sank to rise no more, and he was one of Moffatt's men. One of our expert swimmers dived in to search for the body, which was found after half an hour, placed in a dinghy at our stern and covered with straw, for we intended to bury him on reaching Bruges. On arrival there, Moffatt and I called on the Mayor, who informed us that the nearest burying ground was three miles away; so, as it was already late, we took his advice, which was to carry it on to Ostend.

Meanwhile, we went to an English hotel, where we found a number of our countrymen dining, and as we had had no refreshment for several hours we joined the throng. We were entertained also by musicians and Morris dancers, quite a few of whom seemed to support themselves in this way. We retired late, having difficulty in finding a bed, but were up again at 4.0 to search for our men and continue our journey.

We reached Ostend early on the 24th and reported to the Commandant, who happened to be Colonel Burton of the 7th

Fusiliers. He ordered us to make arrangement for the corpse to be interred without delay, and prepare to embark promptly for England as Lieutenant Meyer's detachment of the King's German Legion also intended to sail next day. The place was terribly crowded, but I obtained a billet at last, though a very indifferent one.

CHAPTER 20

From Deal to Donington

On Friday 25 August, Lieutenant Meyer of the King's German Legion, Moffatt of the 71st, and I, with our three detachments, boarded the *Elizabeth* transport.[1] The weather being fine, we sailed under a moderate breeze and were on our way before 3.0. The wind then increased, enabling us to make rapid progress, and we arrived near Deal by 2.0 next morning. By 8.0 we had landed, and after breakfast at *The Royal Exchange*, called at the Transport Office to leave our Returns. On confirming their receipt, a private of dragoons was sent to Canterbury, Headquarters of the District, for further orders.

By 7.0 on the 27th we had heard from Captain Mancour, the Commandant at Deal, that he had received orders that all three detachments should be disembarked and placed in the South Infantry Barracks. Together with Meyer and Moffatt, I went aboard the *Elizabeth*, which had moored about a mile from the shore. Boats were provided to land them, and by 10.0 they were all in the barracks. A room each was allotted to us. As these were Field Officers Quarters, we took our meals there also.

I drew the Subsistence Allowance daily from Captain Mancour for the men we had brought in, and was then ordered to give them their Discharges and pay them their Marching Allowances.

---

1   This could have been 12-gun schooner HMS *Elizabeth*.

The following is the declaration I signed when the Acquittance Roll was settled:

Deal,

10 Sept., 1815

I do declare upon my honor that I have paid to all the men forming the detachment that was placed under my command at Neuilly on 11 August 1815 from the 4th, 27th, and the 29th regiments all the money that was due to them from their respective regiments, for which they have each signed their names and made no complaints.

Robert Bakewell, 27th Regiment

Commanding the Detachment

(Pay Bill of the Detachment to be inserted here)

Having finally settled with the Detachment as far as my responsibility was concerned, I began to the settle my own accounts before my departure from Deal. When I had paid all the claims against me – including that of the mess-man of the 4th Regiment – I found myself short, having only a few shillings left; but what else could be expected, as I had not been getting the usual allowances. An ensigncy's pay is but a pittance when considering the expenses of an officer's march through such a country as England. Although I could not obtain from the Secretary of War either the grant or any reason why I was not to receive it, I found that those subalterns who had returned with the actual battalion had done soon afterwards and without difficulty.

However, Mancour proposed cashing a draft for me upon our Agent for £20. By the morning of 12 September I was ready to make a fresh start. After walking nineteen miles to Canterbury, I put up at *The Fleur de Lis* inn, next morning calling on Mr McDonald, the Paymaster of the district (the town being the headquarters of this jurisdiction), and handed him the Acquittance Roll and Pay Bill of the detachment, so that he could examine them and check that those accounts agreed with the monies drawn by Captain Mancour.

At 1.0 next day, Moffatt and I took the coach for London. We dined at Rochester, a bustling place, being on the direct road to the Channel Ports, through which passed a great deal of traffic. The landlord of the inn squeezes his transient guests too much: we were charged 5s and 6d each for our dinners, exclusive of beer, wine, etc., and he gave us hardly sufficient time to digest it. However, we reached London that evening; alighted from the stage; and took a hackney coach for the *Angel Inn*, but were driven to another 'Angel Inn' behind St Clements instead of that in Angel Street, St Martin's Le Grand, to which we then made our way.

Next day, we went to the Drury Lane theatre, and on the 15th I called on General Torrens,[2] the Commander-in-Chief's Military Secretary, and also on Mr Ridge, the Agent, where I found that he had paid my £20 on account.

Here, I met some of the men forming my detachment demanding clothing allowances, etc., but such an irregular body of merry fellows could rarely be found together. Apparently, from Deal and through Canterbury and Rochester, the turnpike was strewn with them, as were the fields adjoining, where they enjoyed the company of the girls they had picked up as partners, and all of them were as intoxicated as liquor could make them. As might be expected, by the time they had reached London they found their money gone, their fair friends having taken the opportunity of relieving them of all that they had not already spent.

---

2   Major General Sir Henry Torrens (1779–1828), had been Military Secretary to the Commander-in-Chief since 1809; and in 1820 became Adjutant General to the forces.

To obtain a fresh supply was their only object; but to do so it was necessary that each should show their discharge papers to their regiment's Agent before they could effectively demand Prize Money and any Clothing Allowance which might be due to them; but hardly one of them had such a paper in their possession or indeed any knowledge of what they should have produced. Some had those of their comrades; others had secured three or four; the rest could only admit that they had lost them. Eventually, the Agent collected the men together, gave them new discharge papers and settled their demands. But hardly had he done so when the majority started carousing until, again, all was spent. They then applied to me with the intention of re-enlisting.

I contacted Captain [name undecipherable], who lived in Kensington, stationed there on recruiting service, to ask whether he would enlist them, thinking that it might be advantageous to the Service, they being veterans and well disciplined; but he informed me that his orders had been to enlist none aged over thirty. As all this crew were between thirty and forty, he suggested I referred the matter to the Adjutant General, to whom I then applied, but the answer was that he could not deviate from this regulation. Naturally, this was unwelcome news when I made it known the men; but at this juncture all I could do was to take my leave of them, with the hope that they would make their way to their respective homes as best they could.

I then called at the Superintendent's Office for Military Accounts in Westminster, where I obtained my Acquittance. All was found to be correct.

*

At this point, after dining with a Captain Wilson, who lived in Leigh Street, Burton Crescent, and who had formerly assisted him, Bakewell involved himself in correspondence to get an appointment on the Veteran establishment, but was unsuccessful. Having completed all necessary duties — except that he had not yet received any orders as to where he should now report — Bakewell decided to leave London.

Before doing so, he penned another letter to the Adjutant General from 44 Charing Cross, dated 21 September 1815, requesting two or three months' leave of absence. The reply granted him such leave until 24 October, but stipulated that any application to extend it beyond that date would have to be made to the Commanding Officer of the battalion to which he belonged.

Bakewell was detained in London until the 23rd, when he took coach from The White Horse, Fetter Lane. Passing through St Albans, Dunstable, Woburn, and Northampton, it stopped at The Angel Inn, Leicester, where he remained two days before continuing his journey through Loughborough to Lockington. From there, he walked the short distance to Castle Donington, reached on the evening of 26 September, 1815.

He remained there until Friday, 3 November 1815,when he hired a gig to Derby, staying overnight at The Nag's Head, and next day took a coach — changing horses at Uttoxeter, Newcastle-under-Lyme, and Nantwich — for Chester, and The White Lion. On the following day, he crossed the Mersey from Eastham Bay to Liverpool, arriving there in the late afternoon, and put up at the Commercial Inn: he should not have to wait long for the Dublin packet.

Indeed, he was soon well on his way to Ballyshannon, still the headquarters of the 2nd Battalion of the 27th Regiment. The 3rd Battalion was disbanded in the following January. Bakewell himself was placed on half-pay on 25 July 1817.

But we must now take our leave, for here ends that volume of his Diary. Robert Bakewell lived on for another thirty-seven years, dying on 24 February 1853 in his seventy-seventh year at Castle Donington, where, in the central table tomb outside the south door of the church of St Edward, King and Martyr, he now lies. Requiescat in pace.

Selective Bibliography

I TRUST I WILL BE forgiven for not including numerous other favourites – Robert Blakeney, John Cooke, William Grattan, William Green, Benjamin Harris, John Kincaid, Jonathan Leach, George Simmons, and William Surtees, to mention only half a dozen or so at random – as I wanted to list only those whose titles I felt were particularly relevant to the actions, regiment, and subjects referred to; thus, the general histories of Napier and Fortescue are not referred to and, doubtless, several other deserving titles have been unintentionally overlooked.

Aitchison, John (ed. W. F. K. Thompson), *An Ensign in the Peninsular War* (1981)

Anon., (The Regimental Historical Records Committee), *The Royal Inniskilling Fusiliers 1688–1914* (revised edition 1934; reprinted 2010 by the Naval and Military Press)

Barratt, C. R. B., *History of the 13th Hussars* (1911)

Bingham (ed. Gareth Glover), *Wellington's Lieutenant, Napoleon's Gaoler: The Peninsular and St Helena diaries and letters of Sir George Ridout Bingham, 1809–21* (2004)

Boutflower, Charles, *The Journal of an Army Surgeon during the Peninsular War* (1912; reprinted 1997)

Bragge, William (ed. S. A. C. Cassels), *Peninsular Portrait, 1811–1814: The Letters of Captain William Bragge* (1963)

Brett-James, Antony, *Life in Wellington's Army* (1972; reprinted 1994)

Brooke, William; see Oman

Burgoyne (ed. Hon. George Wrottesley), *The Life and Correspondence of F.M. Sir John Burgoyne*, Bart. (1873)

Burnham, Robert, *Charging against Wellington: The French Cavalry in the Peninsular War 1807–1814* (2011)

Cassidy, Martin, *Marching with Wellington: with the Inniskillings in the Napoleonic Wars* (2003)

Cole, Maud Lowry and Stephen Gwyn (eds.), *Memoirs of Sir Lowry Cole* (1934; reprinted 2003)

Colville, John, *The Portrait of a General* (1980), that of the Hon. Sir Charles Colville

Cooper, John Spencer, *Rough Notes of Seven Campaigns* (1869; reprinted 1996)

Costello, Edward, *The Adventures of a Soldier* (1841); as *The Peninsular War and Waterloo Campaigns* (ed. Antony Brett-James; 1967), and much extended as *Costello: the True Story of a Peninsular War Rifleman* (ed. Eileen Hathaway; 1997)

Crowe, Charles (ed. Gareth Glover), *An Eloquent Soldier: The Peninsular War Journals of Lientenant Charles Crowe of the Inniskillings, 1813–1814* (2011)

Crumplin, Michael, *Men of Steel: Surgery in the Napoleonic Wars* (2007)

——— *Guthrie's War: a Surgeon of the Peninsula and Waterloo* (2010)

D'Urban, Sir Benjamin (ed. I. J. Rousseau), *The Peninsular Journal* (1930; reprinted 1988)

Dempsey, Guy, *Albuera 1811* (2008)

Dickson, Alexander, *The Dickson Manuscripts* (1905; reprinted 1987)

Edwards, Peter, *Albuera: Wellington's Fourth Peninsular Campaign, 1811* (2008)

Emerson; see Maxwell

Fletcher, Ian, *Galloping at Everything* (1999), for Campo Maior

Frazer (ed. Edward Sabine), *Letters of Colonel Sir Augustus Simon Frazer, KCB commanding the Royal Horse Artillery in the army under Wellington* (1859; reprinted 2001)

Fryer, Mary (ed.), *Our Young Soldier; Lieutenant Francis Simcoe, 6 June 1791–6 April 1812* (Toronto, 1996)

Gordon, Alexander (ed. Rory Muir), *At Wellington's Right Hand: The Letters of Lieutenant-Colonel Sir Alexander Gordon, 1808–1815* (2003)

Green, William (eds. J. and D. Teague), *Where My Duty Calls Me* (1975)

Hall, John A., *The Biographical Dictionary of British Officers Killed and Wounded, 1808–1814* (vol. VIII, added to the Greenhill Books reprint of Oman's *History*; 1998)

Henry, Walter, *Surgeon Henry's Trifles: Events of a Military Life* (1970; reprinted 2011)

Howard, Martin, *Wellington's Doctors* (2002)

Inside Wellington's Peninsular War Army, 1808–1814, by Rory Muir, Robert Burnham, Howie Muir, and Ron McGuigan (2006), notably for the article on 'Bridging Operations'

Lawrence, William (ed. Eileen Hathaway), *A Dorset Soldier: the Autobiography of Sergeant William Lawrence* (1993)

Long, Robert B. (ed. T. H. McGuffie), *Peninsular Cavalry General* (1951)

Maxwell, William Hamilton (ed.), *Peninsular Sketches; by Actors on the Scene*, vol. 2 (1845; reprinted 1998) contains a short piece (pp. 205–42) by Private John Emerson of the Inniskillings, concerning the aborted siege of Badajoz, and Albuera

Muir, Rory, *Britain and the Defeat of Napoleon, 1807–1815* (1996)

Oman, Sir Charles, *Wellington's Army* (1913; reprinted 1986)

—— *Studies in the Napoleonic Wars* (1929; reprinted 1989) contains Major William Brooke's 'A Prisoner of Albuera'

—— *A History of the Peninsular War* (1902–30: reprinted 1996), particularly vol. IV

Robertson, Ian, *A Commanding Presence: Wellington in the Peninsula: Logistics, Strategy, Survival* (2008)

——*An Atlas of the Peninsular War* (Yale, 2010, with cartography by Martin Brown)

Sherer, Moyle, *Recollections of the Peninsula* (1824; reprinted 1996 with an Introduction by Philip J. Haythornthwaite)

Simcoe, Francis; see Fryer

Stanhope, James (ed. Gareth Glover), *Eyewitness to the Peninsular War and the Battle of Waterloo: The Letters and Journals of Lieutenant Colonel the Hon. James Stanhope* (2010)

Stanhope, Philip Henry, *Notes of Conversations with the Duke of Wellington 1831–1851*(1888)

Tomkinson, William (ed. James Tomkinson), *The Diary of a Cavalry Officer in the Peninsular War and Waterloo Campaign, 1808–1815* (1895; reprinted 1971)

Trimble, William Copeland, *The historical record of the 27th Inniskilling regiment, from . . . its institution as a volunteer corps till the present time* (1876; reprinted 2003)

Ward, S. G. P., *Wellington's Headquarters: a Study of the Administrative Problems in the Peninsula, 1809–1814* (1957)

Weller, Jac [John Allen Claude] (ed. Ian Robertson), *Wellington in the Peninsula* (1962)

Wheeler, William (ed. B.H. Liddell Hart), *The Letters of Private Wheeler, 1809–1828* (1951; reprinted 1994)

Addenda

The reader's attention is drawn also to Susan L Siegfried's *The Art of Louis-Léopold Boilly: Modern Life in Napoleonic France* (Yale, 1995) and *Boilly 1761–1845* (Editions Nicolas Chaudrun, 2011), both providing vivid visual images of Paris at that period.

Index

Bakewell's narrative touches on a wide variety of subjects, many described more *en passant* than in detail, but the majority of places referred to have been included; however, establishing the Christian name, regiment and rank of every officer at the time that each is mentioned has posed problems, largely due to lapses in transcription and, despite trawling through the Challis List (among other sources), some inevitably remain unresolved.